101 Playmakers and Special Plays

The Complete Coaches' Playbook of Innovative Plays

Charlie Stubbs

COACHES CHOICE™

ISBN: 978-1-60679-083-0
Library of Congress Control Number: 2009944036

Book layout: Bean Creek Studio
Cover design: Brenden Murphy
Front and back cover photos: Sports Information Department—University of Alabama

Coaches Choice
P.O. Box 1828
Monterey, CA 93942
www.coacheschoice.com

Dedication

To my wife, Sandy—my best friend. Together we have shared the triumphs and disappointments of a coaching career. I also dedicate this book to my grandchildren: Isaac, Addisyn, Elsa, Bradley, and Lucas… and still counting. Their boundless energy and enthusiasm help keep this old coach forever young, and their unconditional love reminds me that football is just a game.

Acknowledgments

The completion of this book was made possible through the encouragement and teamwork of a number of people.

I wish to thank the following friends in the coaching profession: Robert Anae, Fisher DeBerry, Mike Empey, Scott Grinde, Jeff Horton, Dave Kragthorpe, Noel Mazzone, Danny Pearman, Homer Smith, Dabo Swinney, and Bob Toledo. All contributed special plays for this project. I especially want to thank my son, Troy Stubbs, for writing the foreword.

I am deeply grateful to Jeff Conway, who used his gifts to skillfully draw the plays and assist with the organization of the special plays DVD.

My special thanks is also expressed to the staff at Coaches Choice, particularly Dr. Jim Peterson for giving me another opportunity to give something back to the profession.

Finally, I would like to acknowledge all of the great coaches and players that I have had the opportunity to work with. Without you this book would not be possible.

Perfection is our goal but excellence will be tolerated.

Foreword

Innovative plays are not a new concept in football. In fact, as a ten-year-old boy in the late 1980's, I was in the midst of great coaches and players, enjoying the game day atmosphere and the thrill of exciting plays on the field. Each Saturday, I held the headset cord for my dad on the sidelines of PAC-10 games. As I shared my own dreams of playing and coaching college football, the players and coaches accepted me as part of the team and were always respectful and encouraging. Once I grew to be a teenager, I became more observant and began to understand that football games were not simply a Saturday event. I witnessed my father spend countless hours watching film, scripting practices, and formulating game plans. My personal interest level in the details of offensive football began to grow, and my questions were very specific. While a "sideline assistant" for my dad at Oregon State University, I resolved to one day be a college football coach.

The path to fulfilling my dream of becoming a college football coach is different than most. After playing for Coach Fisher DeBerry for two years at the United States Air Force Academy, I chose to serve a mission for the Church of Jesus Christ of Latter Day Saints in Russia for two years. Upon my return, I transferred to the University of Alabama where my father was coaching. My interests had shifted to business, and by graduation I was married, had a child, and then began a career in investments. Coaching football was an unrealized dream that still lingered in the back of my mind.

Watching the game as an avid fan and spectator, I gravitated toward the exciting, game-changing plays that resulted in passionate "water cooler" conversations among co-workers each Monday morning. It was exceptionally clear to me that electrifying, inventive offenses were the most talked about and popular among fans of football. After four years of eagerly watching from afar, with the support of my wife and family, I joined my father at the University of Louisville as a graduate assistant. This opportunity kicked off my career in coaching college football and provided me with the chance to pursue my dream.

Reflecting on my experience as a youth, player, and spectator, I knew I wanted to incorporate creative play in the development of my own offensive philosophy. Today, as a young coach, I am continually seeking knowledge as I expand my library of offensive plays. *101 Playmakers and Special Plays* provides an excellent resource for coaches at all levels. No matter what your experience level is as a coach, this book will inspire a creative spark in your preparation and game planning as you develop your individual offensive philosophy.

—Troy Stubbs
Quarterback/Running Backs Coach
University of Arkansas at Monticello

Contents

Note: Plays included on the companion DVD are marked with an asterisk.

Dedication 3

Acknowledgments 4

Foreword 5

Introduction 10

Chapter 1: Philosophy and Design of Special Plays and Playmakers 13

Chapter 2: Screens, Fake Screens, and Shovel Passes 25

#1: Fake Zone Right Quick Screen Left (Stubbs, Alabama)*
#2: Wide Receiver Screen Left—Ex. 1 (Stubbs, Alabama)*
#3: Wide Receiver Screen Left—Ex. 2 (Stubbs, Alabama)*
#4: Double Pass Throwback Screen to Quarterback (Horton, Wisconsin)*
#5: Sweep Right Screen Left to Tight End (Stubbs, Oregon State)*
#6: Fake Draw Right Crack Screen Left—Strong (Stubbs, Oregon State)*
#7: Fake Draw Right Crack Screen Left—Weak (Stubbs, Oregon State)*
#8: Zone Left Reverse Right Screen Left to Quarterback (Stubbs, Tulsa)*
#9: Double Pass Screen to Quarterback (Anae, Texas Tech)
#10: Sprint Right Screen Left to Fullback (Stubbs, Tulsa)*
#11: Shift From Unbalanced Formation Double Screen Right (Stubbs, Louisville)*
#12: Double Screen Right With Back Motion (Stubbs, Tulsa)*
#13: Double Screen Right With Hip Motion (Stubbs, UCM)*
#14: Fake Bubble Left Slip Screen Right (Stubbs, Tulsa)*
#15: Fake F Drag Slip Screen Left (Stubbs, Tulsa)*
#16: Pre-Snap Movement Slip Screen Left (Stubbs, Tulsa)*
#17: Sprint Right Throwback Screen Left (Stubbs, UCM)
#18: Rub Screen Right R Go (Stubbs, UCM)
#19: Fun Pass (Stubbs, Alabama)*
#20: Fake Wide Receiver Screen Special—Ex. 1 (Stubbs, Alabama)*
#21: Fake Wide Receiver Screen Special—Ex. 2 (Stubbs, Alabama)*
#22: Flash Double Arc (Stubbs, UCM)
#23: Shovel Pass Right (Stubbs, Alabama)*
#24: Shovel Pass Left (Stubbs, UNLV)*
#25: Shovel Pass With Lead Blocker (Stubbs, UCM)

Chapter 3: Fake Draw Passes **51**
#26: Fake Draw Right All Takeoff (Four Vertical)—Ex. 1 (Stubbs, Tulsa)*
#27: Fake Draw Right All Takeoff (Four Vertical)—Ex. 2 (Stubbs, Tulsa/UCM)*
#28: Fake Draw Right All Takeoff (Four Vertical)—Ex. 3 (Stubbs, Tulsa)*
#29: Fake Draw Right Backs Cross (Stubbs, Alabama)*

Chapter 4: Reverses, Reverse Passes, and Fake Reverse Passes **57**
#30: Counter Right Reverse Left—Weak (Stubbs, Tulsa)*
#31: Counter Right Reverse Left—Strong (Stubbs, UNLV)*
#32: Toss Right Reverse Left (Stubbs, Alabama)*
#33: Zone Right Reverse Left—Ex. 1 (Stubbs, Alabama)*
#34: Zone Right Reverse Left—Ex. 2 (Stubbs, Tulsa)*
#35: Speed Option Right Reverse Left (Stubbs, Tulsa)*
#36: Sweep Right Reverse Left (Horton, Wisconsin)*
#37: Bounce Left Reverse Right (Swinney, Clemson)*
#38: Fake Zone Right Reverse Left (Stubbs, UCM)
#39: Toss Right Reverse Left (Stubbs, UCM)
#40: Fake Iso Reverse Left (Stubbs, UCM)
#41: Fake Zone Left Reverse Right Pass (Stubbs, Alabama)*
#42: Speed Sweep Left Reverse Right Pass (Stubbs, Tulsa)*
#43: Reverse Pass Off Bounce Play (Swinney, Clemson)*
#44: Lead Option Left Reverse Right Pass (Toledo, UCLA)
#45: Zone Right Fake Reverse Pass—Ex. 1 (Stubbs, Alabama)
#46: Zone Right Fake Reverse Pass—Ex. 2 (Stubbs, Alabama)*
#47: Fake Zone and Reverse Wheel Route (Stubbs, Alabama)*
#48: Fake Zone and Reverse Pass (Stubbs, Tulsa)*
#49: Zone Right Fake Reverse H Wheel (Stubbs, Tulsa)*
#50: Fake Lead Left Reverse Throwback (Empey, BYU)*

Chapter 5: Special Play-Action Passes **79**
#51: Toss Right Halfback Pass—Ex. 1 (Stubbs, Alabama)*
#52: Toss Right Halfback Pass—Ex. 2 (Stubbs, UCM)
#53: Fake Draw Running Back Seam (Stubbs, Alabama)*
#54: Fake Iso Right Wheel Route (Stubbs, Tulsa)*
#55: Fake Speed Sweep and Zone Y Sneak (Stubbs, Tulsa)*
#56: Option Right Pass (DeBerry, Air Force Academy)*
#57: Unbalanced Right Zone Right Pass (Empey, BYU)*
#58: Fake Zone Left Z Dagger—Ex. 1 (Stubbs, Louisville)*
#59: Fake Zone Left Z Dagger—Ex. 2 (Stubbs, Louisville)*
#60: Unbalanced Fake Iso Right Firm Dipper (Stubbs, UCM)
#61: Fake Dive Right Double Pass (Stubbs, UCM)

Chapter 6: Special Move the Pocket Plays: Roll-Outs, Bootlegs, and Nakeds. . 91
#62: Dash Right Bomb (Stubbs, Alabama)*
#63: Reach Right Tight End Hide (Stubbs, Tulsa)
#64: Fake Sweep Right Bootleg Left Throwback—Pro-set (Kragthorpe, Oregon State)*
#65: Fake Sweep Right Bootleg Left Throwback—Boundary—Slot Formation (Kragthorpe, Oregon State)*
#66: Zone Left Naked Right Throwback—Ex. 1 (Stubbs, Tulsa)*
#67: Zone Left Naked Right Throwback—Ex. 2 (Stubbs, Tulsa/UCM)*
#68: Zone Left Naked Right Throwback—Ex. 3 (Stubbs, Tulsa)*
#69: Unbalanced Zone Left Naked Right Sail (Stubbs, Louisville)*
#70: Fake Speed Sweep Zone Naked Right Sail (Stubbs, Tulsa)*
#71: Zone Left Naked Right Tube (Stubbs, Louisville)*
#72: Fake Speed Sweep Left Naked Right (Stubbs, Tulsa)
#73: Zone Left Naked Right Throwback (Stubbs, Alabama)*

Chapter 7: Special Formation Plays: Bunch, Stack, Empty 105
#74: Bunch Right Zone Right Fake Reverse Pass Z Over (Mazzone, NC State)
#75: Bunch Right Zone Right Fake Reverse Pass X Over (Mazzone, NC State)
#76: Bunch Zone Right Reverse Left (Stubbs, UCM)*
#77: Stack Formation Smash Route (Stubbs, Alabama)*
#78: Stack Special (Stubbs, Alabama)*
#79: No-Back Quick Pass (Stubbs, Alabama)*
#80: Empty—Three-Man Seams (Smith, UCLA/Alabama)
#81: Empty Pass Double Cross (Stubbs, UCM)*
#82: Empty Pass Takeoff Y Drive (Stubbs, UCM)*
#83: Bench and Up Pass (Stubbs, Alabama)*
#84: H Wheel (Stubbs, Alabama)*

Chapter 8: Special Run Plays **117**
#85: Speed Sweep Right (Stubbs, Tulsa)*
#86: T Right Load Option Left (Stubbs, Alabama)*
#87: Bunch Unbalanced Pitch Left (Stubbs, UCM)*
#88: Change 19 (Outside Zone Left) (Stubbs, UCM)*
#89: Change 14 (Inside Zone Right) (Stubbs, UCM)
#90: Zone Read Left Flash (Stubbs, UCM)*
#91: Zone Read Arc (Stubbs, Tulsa)*
#92: Zone Read Option—Ex. 1 (Stubbs, Tulsa)*
#93: Zone Read Option—Ex. 2 (Stubbs, Tulsa)*
#94: Unbalanced Zone Read Option—Ex. 3 (Stubbs, Tulsa)*
#95: Belly Right Flip Left (Stubbs, UCM)
Chapter 9: Kicking Game Special Plays and Fakes **129**
#96: Punt Team Special (Stubbs, Tulsa)
#97: Reverse Punt Return (Pearman, Virginia Tech)
#98: Kickoff Return Throwback Pass (Pearman, Virginia Tech)
#99: Fake Field Goal Flood Pattern (Pearman, Virginia Tech)
#100: Fake Field Goal Pass (Grinde, UCM)*
#101: Fake Field Goal Shovel Pass (Grinde, UCM)
About the Author **137**

Introduction

The game of football has changed significantly since Rutgers and Princeton played in the first game on November 6, 1869. The game has evolved to include the use of video equipment and high tech computers for the study and breakdown of each play. This advanced study of football by coaches looking for an edge brings new and dynamic ideas to the game. With 11 offensive players, the methods of attack are limited only by the width and length of the field and the coach's imagination. As a student of the game, I find the Xs and Os of football fascinating.

The easiest way to start a conversation with a football coach is to ask about his best play. All coaches have favorite offensive plays. They all have favorite special plays. These preferences lead to the distinctive style of coaching that makes football so exciting.

As part of the weekly offensive game planning, a coach should design special plays. These explosive plays can jump start the team and therefore need to be innovative and able to exploit a defensive weakness or player. When developing the game plan, it is important to identify the team's playmakers. Playmakers are those athletes who must have the ball in their hands a major portion of the game for the team to be successful.

When I first considered writing this book, I believed that a compilation of outstanding, game changing plays would be a great asset to a coach's resources. The plays included in this book come from my coaching experiences and contributions from fellow coaches. The coaches represented have many years of successful coaching and are outstanding teachers. As you read this book, I believe you will be exposed to numerous thoughts, concepts, and principals for developing a championship team. In addition, I hope this book will be an invaluable reference text for players, coaches, and even the fan or football enthusiast.

101 Playmakers and Special Plays will benefit coaches at all levels as they strive to utilize their playmakers properly and jump start their team with special plays. Included with the book are 101 plays with complete diagrams, descriptions, and assignments for each position player. Also included is a companion DVD featuring actual game footage of 76 of these special plays being executed at a high level. The DVD will give coaches a visual example of the plays and the playmakers as they compete against various defensive schemes. The video clips span the past three decades. Coaches will notice the evolution of football during that time period. In fact, a few of the clips have been transferred from the original 16 mm film. I really enjoyed making this DVD and collection of plays. It brought back many fond memories.

I am a product of many coaches, learning from them all—while at the same time trying to add my own innovations and adjustments to give the players a better chance for success. I am hopeful that this book will be extremely useful to you, regardless of your basic system or philosophy. The best coaches are always looking for a way to gain the competitive edge. It just may be that a play from this book could help your team win a crucial game. Then my efforts to write this book would have been worthwhile.

1

Philosophy and Design of Special Plays and Playmakers

University of Central Missouri Sports Information Department

An effective offensive package is complemented with special plays and playmakers. These two additions can be the difference between an average team or a championship team. Properly utilized and managed, special plays and playmakers make an offense explosive, exciting, and highly successful. This chapter will address special plays, playmakers, and a philosophy to consider assisting in maintaining the proper balance between these elements and the rest of the offense.

Special Plays

"All warfare is based upon deception."

—Sun-Tzu, Chinese Military Strategist, *The Art of War*

Special plays are intended to provide the element of surprise and cause defensive confusion. Within the weekly offensive game plan, a coach should design special plays. These plays can jump-start an offense, and therefore need to be innovative and able to exploit a defensive weakness or defensive player. Specials need to be set up properly and called at the correct time.

Numerous factors must be taken into account when considering the design of special plays, as well as the timing of when they should be called. Considering the following factors can aid coaches in their efforts to develop this unique package:

- Most successful specials complement a core/base offensive play that a team has in its offensive plan.
- A variety of formations/motions/personnel groupings should be used to help in disguising the play from game to game. Special plays will quickly lose their effectiveness when overused.
- A coach should give these plays enough practice preparation. Repetitions are the keys to offensive success.

"Don't mistake activity for achievement. Practice it the right way."

—John Wooden, Hall of Fame Basketball Coach, UCLA

- Timing is paramount. A special play called at the proper time can mean the difference between a win and a loss. Using a special play early in the game is a great opportunity to jump-start the offense and the team. Another good time to use a special play is on a change of possession or after a big play when the defense is rattled or confused.
- Special plays are designed to exploit a defensive tendency or weakness, or a particular defensive player.

Other factors coaches should consider include:

✓Down-and-distance

✓Field location (e.g., red zone, hash)

✓Time of game (e.g., first/fourth quarter, before the half)

Sample Situation: A coach has a wide receiver (Z) on his team that is a playmaker. The coach believes the wide receiver will get limited touches within the base offense through the passing game but wants to ensure additional opportunities during the flow of the game. Figures 1-1 to 1-4 provide examples of special plays utilized to get the playmaker more involved.

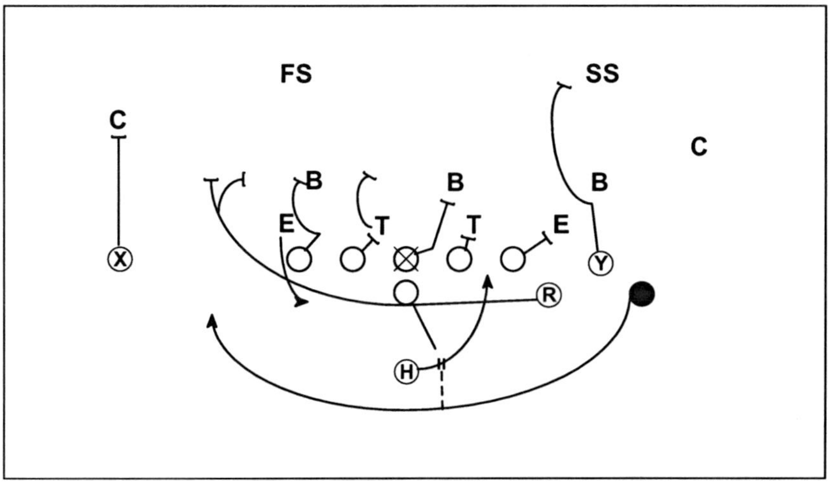

Figure 1-1. Special reverse: (S) trey right bunch zone right reverse left

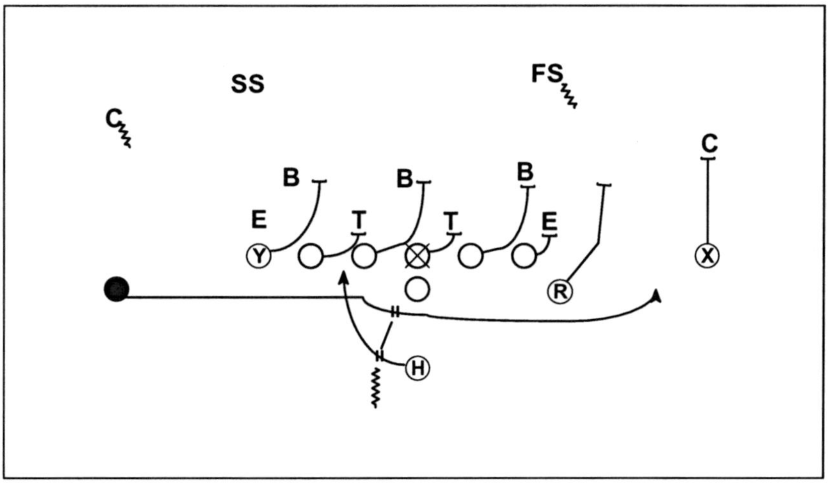

Figure 1-2. Special run: (S) up left zoom speed sweep right

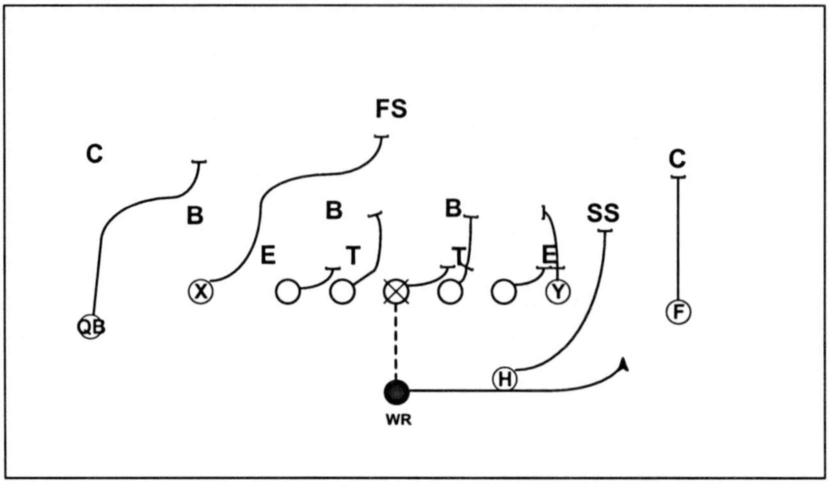

Figure 1-3. Special run (change package): (D) purple right change 18

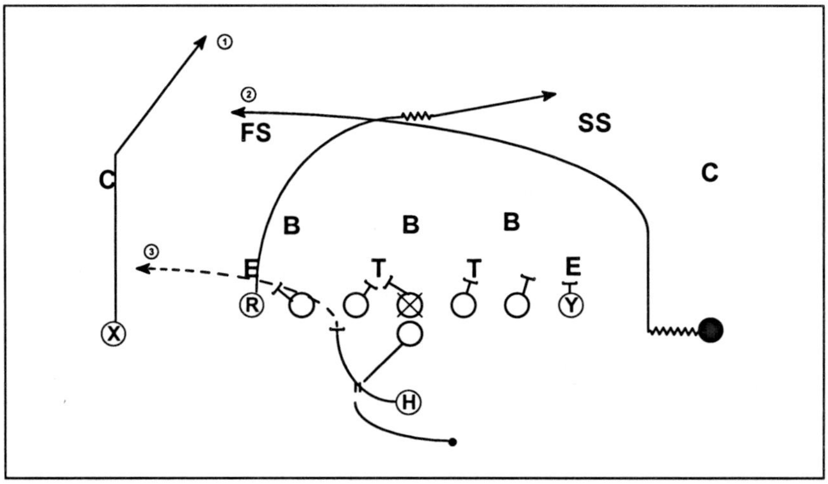

Figure 1-4. Special deep play-action pass: (A) right zing zone left naked right Z dagger

Game Week Preparation

Installation of Special Plays

Once you have determined—after much video study of the opponent—that a certain special play will be great in attacking a particular defensive player or scheme, you need to practice it. In practice #1 of game week, the coaches and players should work on the specific parts of the play (e.g., reverse action, double-pass technique). In practice #2, the entire offense should execute the play against a scout team that will give the exact look needed multiple times. At this time the players will understand why the play works and will gain confidence in the play with great execution. In practices #3 and #4, the play should be inserted into the team script at the proper situation (down/distance, hash, yard line, etc.) that it will be utilized in the game. The offense should only run the play once each day to make them understand that on most special plays you only get one opportunity to make it happen—no repeats!

Aggressive Play Caller With a Big Play Offense

Of course, after proper preparation with video study, meetings, and practice, you must be confident as a coach about your offensive game plan. As a play caller, during the last couple of days of game week, the coach has already played the game in his mind many times over so he will be prepared to react in various situations to make the proper play call. When utilizing special plays, the play caller must go with his instinct, with no hesitation. The coach cannot second-guess or worry about negative consequences. To make things happen, you must have the courage to make the call that will give your players an opportunity to make a big play.

"The coach must have a definite plan in which he believes, and there must be no compromise on his part."

—Paul "Bear" Bryant, Hall of Fame Football Coach, University of Alabama

Playmakers

When developing the offensive plan, it is important to identify the team's *playmakers*, the athletes who must have the ball in their hands a major portion of the game for the team to be successful. The goal should be to get the ball to the playmakers in at least two-thirds of all offensive plays. The playmaker title is earned through hard work and production in practice and games. Many successful coaches design specific plays beyond the core offense to allow these gifted athletes to use their skills. Remember: *Players make plays!*

Game Planning

Game planning is an ongoing process throughout the week. Time should be spent wisely in meetings, studying video, executing drills, and then viewing practice video. A good coach leaves no stone unturned. All situations must be covered, including goal line/short yardage, red zone, two-point plays, special plays, and the two-minute offense.

The coordinator/play caller should work on the game-day play-call form (refer to Figure 1-5) throughout the week, making minor adjustments after each practice. All decisions should be made at least 24 hours before the game. A good offensive coordinator will have played the game in his mind many times before the team steps on the field. He must study his opponent and know how it will react in certain situations, leaving no chance for surprises.

GAME PLAN vs: **DATE** ____________________

SCRIPT

1 (F) Purple X Grab/ Double Grab
2 ((S) Trey Bunch Ret. 42 / 43 Dummy
3 (F) Purple 'C' Leo Hooks or
4 (F) Gold Fob 4/5 Read Option
5 Slip Screen (Various)
6 (T) Tan Jet 4/5
7 (F) Purple Stack Smash or
8 (F) Gold Hip Reach Rub
9 (D-Spec) Purple Zoom Speed Sweep
10 (S) Trey Zing 4/5 Dummy
11 (F) Gold B/C Motion 4/5 Read
12 (S) Tan (Unb.) 24 Power

Deep Ball: 1.(A) Left Zing Act 5 Throwback
2. (A) Right Zing Act 5 Z Dagger
3. (S) Mix Eagle 366/367 H Wheel

3RD & 7

1 (A) Right Hip 160 Out
2 (F) Purple 62/63 X Grab/ Double Grab
3 (F) Purple Stack62/63 Smash
4 (A) Zoom to Trips 63/62 Double Cross
5 (D) Fly to Bronze 63/62 X Drive

Screens: 1. (S) Eagle Lt. Zing Slip Screen
2. (A) Trips Lt. Zing Slip Screen Lt.
3. (D) Fly to Bronze Reno R/L

BIG PLAYS

1 (A) Left Zing Act 5 Throwback
2 (A) Right Zing Act 5 Z Dagger
3 (D) Motion to Bronze A/D T.O. X Drive
4 (S) 'T' Load Option R/L
5 (S) Trey Right Zing 4 Reverse

GOAL LINE

FRONTS
RUN

1 (T) Eagle Race 43/42
2 (T) Tan Jet 4/5
3 (T) Eagle Race 4/5 Caddy
4 (TEX) Tan 8/9 (On Set)
5 Special:(Ju) Black Rt Mix 99 Load
6 (Ju) Up Rt. C.C. Load Option

BLITZ

COVERAGE
PASS

1 (S) Trey Bunch Omaha X Slant
2 (T) Tan Rt. Zing Nock 6 Z Snag
3 (A) Trips Close 63/62 Double Cross
4 (H) Black Rt. Slot Aggie 5 Naked Sail

+4 YL Runs

1 (S) Tan Rt. Unb. 24 Power
2 (S) Trey Bunch Ret. 42/43 Dummy
3 (S-Spec) Eagle Change 18/19
4 (D) Mix Bronze 5/4 Read Arc

+4 Passes

1 (S) Eagle Zing 62/63 Z Drive
2 (D) Bronze Close 63/62 Dbl Cross
3 (F) Gold Hip Reach Rub

4th INCHES (T) Eagle Race 43/42 or C.C. Load Opt.

NORMAL DOWNS

RUNS

ONE BACK

1 4/5 (Various) (Color Combo)
2 4/5 Dummy/ Smoke
3 4/5 Read
4 4/5 Read Option
5 5/4 Read Arc
6 C.C. Iso/ 42/43 Dummy
7 Pitch
8 Speed Sweep
9 8/9
10 QB Draw/ Reach Draw
11 Special: 18/19

TWO BACK

1 4/5
2 C.C. Dive
3 24 Power
4 C.C. Iso
5 42/43 (Dummy)
6 48/49 Crack
7 4/5 Read Option
8
9
10

P.A.P.

1 5 Naked Sail
2 5 Smoke Naked Sail
3 Act 5 (Will) Throwback
4 Act 5 Z Dagger
5 Nock 6 Z Snag
6 142 Firm Stutter & Go
7 64 Y Corner Z Post
8
9
10

MOVEMENT PASSES **REACH**

1 (F) Gold Hip Reach Rub
2
3

EMPTY PASSES

1 L/R H Drag
2 L/R Sticks/ Hooks
3 L/R T.O. X Drive
4
5

3 STEP

1 Hitch (Key)
2 Omaha X ✓ Me
3 Arrow
4 366/367: H Wheel
5 Sluggo/ Hitch & Go

5 STEP (CONTROL)

1 Out/ Post Corner
2 X/Z Drive
3 Bench/ Smash (Z Poco)
4 Double Cross
5 Double Snag
6 Takeoff (H Delay)
7 Mayday
8 Curl Y Option
9 X Grab/ Double Grab
10 Double Option

SCREENS

1 Double Screen
2 Slip Screen
3 Reno R/L
4
5

THIRD DOWN

3RD 1-2

FRONT BLITZ COV.

MULE PLUG/QUICK COUNT
RUNS

1 (A) Trips 5/4 (Mule Plug)
2 (T) Tan Jet 4/5
3 (S) Trey Bnch Ret. 42/43 Dummy
4 (T) Eagle Race 43/42
5 (S-Special) 18/19 Change
6 (S) Trey Zing 4/5 Dummy

PASS

1 (T) Tan Zing Nock 6 Z Snag
2 (S) Omaha X ✓ w/ Me
3 (H) Aggie 5 Naked Sail
4 (F) Gold Hip Reach Rub

DEEP: Act 5 Will Throwback

Screen:
(A) Black Unb. Shift Dbl Screen Rt.

3RD 3-5

FRONT BLITZ COV.

MULE PLUG/QUICK COUNT
RUNS (+3)

1 (S) Trey Bch Return 42/43 Dummy
2 (S) Black Unb. C.C. Iso
3 Pitch or 48/49 Crack
4 (T) Tan Jet 4/5
5 (S-Spec) 18/19 Change
6 Speed Sweep

Special: (S) 'T' Load Option

PASS (+3)

1 (F) Purple 'C' Leo Sticks
2 (F) X Grab/ Double Grab
3 62/63 X/Z Drive
4 Omaha X ✓ w/ Me
5 (F) Gold Hip Reach Rub
6 63/62 Double Snag

PASSES (+5)

1 X Grab/ Double Grab
2 63/62 Double Cross
3 (Q) Red 52/53 Smash
4 62/63 X/Z Drive
5 (F) Stack 62/63 Smash
6 (Q) Red 63/62 Double Snag
7 L/R Takeoff X Drive

SCREENS/SPECIALS (+5)

1 Slip Screen (Various)
2 (D-Spec) Purple Zm Spd Sweep
3 (F) L/R H Drag (+3)
4 366/367 H Wheel
5

3RD 6-8

FRONT BLITZ COV.

RUNS (+5)

1 4/5 Read Option
2 4/5 Read Arc
3 (D-Spec) Speed Sweep
4 (F) Gold Reach Rt. Draw
5 (F) QB Draw (Red Zone)

3RD & 7 (Passes)

1 (A) Right Hip 160 Out
2 X Grab/ Double Grab
3 (F) Stack Smash
4 63/62 Double Cross
5 (Q) Red 52/53 Out
6 (D) Purple 60/61 Double Opt
7 62/63 X/Z Drive

3RD & +9

1 (D) Purple 62 Smash Z Poco
2 (A) Right Hip 160 Out
3 (Q) Mot Red 52/53 P-Corner
4 (D) Bronze A/D T.O. X Drive
5 (F) Gold 62/63 T.O. H Delay

Cover 2

1. (D)Purple 60/61 Dbl Option
2. (D)Purple 62 Smash Z Poco
3. (Q) Red 52/53 P. Corner

SCREENS/SPECIALS

1 (A) Trips Zing Slip Screen
2 (S) Eagle Zing Slip Screen
3 (D) Fly to Bronze Reno R/L
4
5

Figure 1-5. Sample game-day play-call form

RED ZONE

+20 Y.L.

RUN (FRONTS)		BLITZ (COV. PASS)
1 (S) Trey B. Ret. 42/43 Dummy	1	63/62 Double Cross
2 Pitch or 48/49 Crack	2	63/62 Double Snag
3 (T) Tan Jet 4/5	3	X Grab/ Double Grab
4 (Q) Black C.C. Dive	4	63/62 X/Z Drive
5 (S) Trey Zing 4/5 Dummy	5	(A) Right Hip 160 Out
6 4/5 Read (Option)	6	(F) Stack 62/63 Smash
7 (D) Purple/ Bronze Off C.C Iso		

P.A.P./3 STEP		SCREENS/SPECIALS
		Special: (S) 'T' Load Option R/L
1 (F) Gold 362/363 Hitch Key	1	Slip Screen (Various)
2 (S)Omaha X ✓ Me	2	(A) Black Unb. Shift Dbl. Scr. Rt.
3 (F) Fly Gold 5 Smoke Naked Sail	3	(D-Spec) Change 18/19
4 (F) Gold Hip Reach Rub	4	Speed Sweep (Various)
5	+25-30:	1. Act 5 (Will) Throwback
6 Draw: (F) Gold Reach Draw		2. (T) Black Rex 64 Takeoff
		3. (S) Mix Eagle 366/367 H Wheel

+10 Y.L.

RUN (FRONTS) *Mule Plug (+10)		BLITZ (COV. PASS)
1 (T) Tan Jet 4/5	1	Trips Close 63/62 Double Cross
2 (S) Tan (Unbalanced) 24 Power	2	(D) Bronze Close63/62 Dbl Cross
3 (S) Trey Bunch Ret. 42/43 Dummy	3	(S) Up Race 63/62 X Drive
4 Pitch/ 48/49 Crack	4	(S) Eagle Zing 62/63 Z Drive
5 (F) Fly to Gold 4/5 Smoke	5	(S) Eagle Zing 62/63 Dbl. Snag
6 4/5 Read (Arc)	6	(F) Bronze B/C H Drag

P.A.P./3 STEP		SPECIALS
1 (S) Bunch Omaha X Slant	1	(S-Spec) Zoom Eagle Unb Speed Sweep
2 (S) Bunch Ret. Nock 6 Z Snag	2	(D-Spec) Purple Change 18/19 (1st Hut)
3 (H) Aggie 5 Naked Sail	3	(F) Bronze B/C QB Draw R/L
4 (F) Gold Hip Reach Rub	4	(D) Mix to Bronze 5/4 Read Arc
5 (D) YoYo 362/363 Arrow	5	

COMING OUT

RUN (FRONTS)	BLITZ (COV. PASS)
1 (TEX) Tan 8/9 (On Set)	1 (F) X Grab/ Double Grab
2 (T) Tan Jet 4/5	2 (Q) Red 63/62 Double Snag
3 (S) Black Unbalanced C.C. Iso	3 (A) Right Hip 160 Out
4 (A) Left/Right Zoom 4/5 Smoke	4 (F) Stack 62/63 Smash
5 C.C. Iso/ 42/43 Dummy	5 (F) Purple 'C' Leo Hooks
	Deep: 1 (T) White Lt. Act 5 Will T. Back

Screen: (S) Eagle Zing Slip Screen R/L

GADGETS

1. 4 Reverse (Various)
2. (S) 'T' Load Option R/L
3. (S) Mix to Eagle 366/367 H Wheel
4. Change Package: 18/19
5. (S-Spec) Zoom to Eagle Unbalanced Speed Sweep
6. (A) Trips Lt. Flex 62 Rugby

MILK CLOCK

RUN	PASS
1 4/5 Dummy/ Smoke	1 5 (Smoke) Naked Sail
2 42/43 Dummy/ C.C. Iso	2 362/363 Hitch Key
3 (TEX) Tan 4/5	3 Omaha X ✓ Me
4 (S) Tan Unb. 24 Power	4 X Grab/ Double Grab
5 Pitch	5 Double Snags
6 Speed Sweep (Various)	6 (F) Stack Smash

Special: 18/19 (Change) Screens: Slip Screen

TWO POINT PLAYS

1. (Ju) Black Mix 99 Load/(D) Mix to Bronze Lt. 4 Read Arc
2. (S) Eagle Zing 62/63 Z Drive
3. (T) Tan Rt. Zing Nock 6 Z Snag/ (D-Spec) Purple Lt. Change 19 (1st Hut)

VICTORY OFFENSE

1. (T) Red Victory
2. (F) Gold 60/61 Flutie/ Flutie Sail

CRITICAL SITUATIONS

LAST PLAY	25 SECONDS 1ST & 10
+20 (D/F) Purple Rt. Smash (Z Poco)	1 (Q) 52/53 Smash/ Out/ P. Corner
+15 (F) Purple Stack 62/63 Smash	2 62/63 X Grab/ Double Grab
+10 (D) Bronze Close 63/62 Dbl Cross	3 62/63 X/Z Drive
+5 (S) Eagle Zing 62/63 Z Drive	4 62/63 Mayday

TWO MINUTE OFFENSE: READY LIST

RUNS	PASSES 362/363	PASSES 62/63	
4/5	Hitch	Bench	Sticks/ Hooks
Personnel: Flush/ Diamond	Fade	Smash	Mayday
Formation: Purple (Flex)		Option	X Grab
		Takeoff	

KEY TERMS: Quick (362 Prot.) Kill, Subway, Clock FG, Bullseye

NOTES: (Q/H) Red Flex 352/353 Shotgun (4th & 6)

Reminders:
1. Clock FG
2. Lock
3. Offense Take a Safety
   (T) Eagle Reach Rt.

HOME RUNS

1. Act 5 (Will) Throwback (Various)
2. (S) Black Rt. 142 Firm Stutter & Go
3. Act 5 Z Dagger (Various)
4. 64 Takeoff (Various- 4 Vertical)
5. (D/F) Purple Right 62 Smash Z Poco
6. (H) Tan Rt. Slot 64 Y Corner Z Post

Figure 1-5. Sample game-day play-call form (cont.)

It is good practice to script the first 10 to 12 plays of the game and emphasize different personnel groupings, formations, motions, and shifts so the coach can see how the defense reacts. The offense should run the scripted plays in a walk-through practice the day before the game. This walk-through lets the players know what to expect, helps the offense be confident of their assignments, and guarantees that the ball will be in the playmakers' hands.

It is very important to organize practices and establish game plans that cover all elements of the game. Organized practices and game plans will reflect directly on a team's success. How a team prepares has a correlation to how the team will play.

Playmaker Touches

During games it is a good idea to assign a specific coach (in the press box) to chart the number of touches the playmakers have to ensure that the offense will not get off course. A form that can be used for this purpose is shown in Figure 1-6. On this form the assistant coach will record the plays that are directed towards a particular playmaker by jersey number. In the passing game, if the playmaker is the first read of that pattern, the coach will record that play. Note: Results of the play will be included and the play caller will refer to the chart numerous times during the game.

Putting It All Together

There is no *one* way to utilize specials and playmakers. Each coach must decide how to best insert the special plays to give his team the greatest chance for success. The same is true for highlighting the talents of the playmakers on your team. Coaching a successful team is very complex and requires organization and dedication to a philosophy. You must work to achieve the balance that brings success to your team. Philosophy includes not only the X's and O's of football but a coach's beliefs about attitude, motivation, and talent.

Attitude

Generally, athletes come to you with an attitude that has already been developed. As a coach, you can fine-tune it but more than likely it will be very difficult to change it. An athlete's positive attitude may be displayed as a good work ethic, a willingness to be a team player, a constant desire to improve, or outstanding leadership qualities. The individual and collective positive attitudes of the team can become the force that drives a team to strive for the highest goals. People don't have good attitudes because they succeed; teams don't have good attitudes because they win. They succeed because of their superior attitudes, because of the way they think, and because of how they align and prioritize their goals. Quality coaches shape this positive enthusiasm and allow it to spread throughout the team.

PLAYMAKERS FREQUENCY CHART			
Week #1	# 7	# 23	# 86
Touches			
Play Called	1.	1.	1.
	2.	2.	2.
	3.	3.	3.
	4.	4.	4.
	5.	5.	5.
	6.	6.	6.
	7.	7.	7.
	8.	8.	8.
	9.	9.	9.
	10.	10.	10.
	11.	11.	11.
	12.	12.	12.

Figure 1-6. Playmakers frequency chart

Motivation

Motivation will control performance. However, it does not come from a coach's pep talk. The best kind of motivation comes from within. A player's desire to perform at his highest level—every workout, every drill, every snap—shows the kind of motivation a coach dreams of. One of a coach's responsibilities concerning motivation is to showcase the positive and downplay the negative. Much has been said about playmakers and the impact they can make in a game and on a team. However, football is a team sport and playmakers must play within the team concept. Coaches have the task of utilizing playmakers in a way that supports the team concept. Care must be taken to properly maintain the balance needed to keep egos in check and motivation high among *all* coaches and players. A playmaker displaying a *healthy* ego (also known as confidence) will help to motivate all his teammates to prepare harder and play harder. A playmaker interested only in promoting himself will quickly lose the support of his team and his contributions to the success of the team will dramatically fall. Former Los Angeles Dodgers manager Tommy Lasorda said it best: "My job is to get these players to play for the name on the front of their jersey, not the number on the back of their jersey!"

Talent

Talent can be divided into two types: the talent you are born with and the talent you utilize. A team's playmakers will be talented athletes, however, they may not necessarily be the most naturally gifted ones. They are simply the athletes who use all their talent and find a way to make things happen. They unselfishly recognize that they are successful because other players on the team did their jobs as well. John Wooden used to say, "The price of glory is the rest of the team," and it is really true of a successful team. It takes every player in every position and every coach performing at his best, without concern for who gets the credit.

There have been teams in the past (and there will be teams in the future) who were talented enough to be championship teams but fell short. They neglected to build the proper foundation needed to support a successful team. The following story illustrates this point.

Day-to-Day Construction
(Author Unknown)

> An elderly carpenter was ready to retire. He told his employer-contractor of his plan to leave the house-building business and live a more leisurely life with his wife, enjoying his extended family. He would miss the paycheck, but he needed to retire. They would get by.
>
> The contractor was sorry to see his good worker go and asked if he could build just one more house as a personal favor. The carpenter said yes, but in time it was easy to see that his heart was not in his work. He resorted to shoddy workmanship and used inferior materials. It was an unfortunate way to end a dedicated

career. When the carpenter finished his work, the employer came to inspect the house. He handed the front door key to the carpenter. "This is your house," he said, "my gift to you."

The carpenter was shocked. What a shame! If he had only known he was building his own house, he would have done it all so differently.

So it is with everyone. They build their lives, a day at a time, often putting less than their best into the building. Then with shock they realize they have to live in the house they have built. If they could do it over, they'd do it much differently. But they cannot go back.

As a coach, you are the carpenter of your team—each time you have a meeting, organize a practice, or install a play. "Life is a do-it-yourself project," someone has said. Your attitudes and the choices you make today build the team you will be tomorrow. Build wisely!

Slogan

Light up the scoreboard.

Motto

Perfection is our goal—but excellence will be tolerated!

2

Screens, Fake Screens, and Shovel Passes

University of Tulsa Sports Information Department

Play #1: Fake Zone Right Quick Screen Left

Charlie Stubbs
University of Alabama

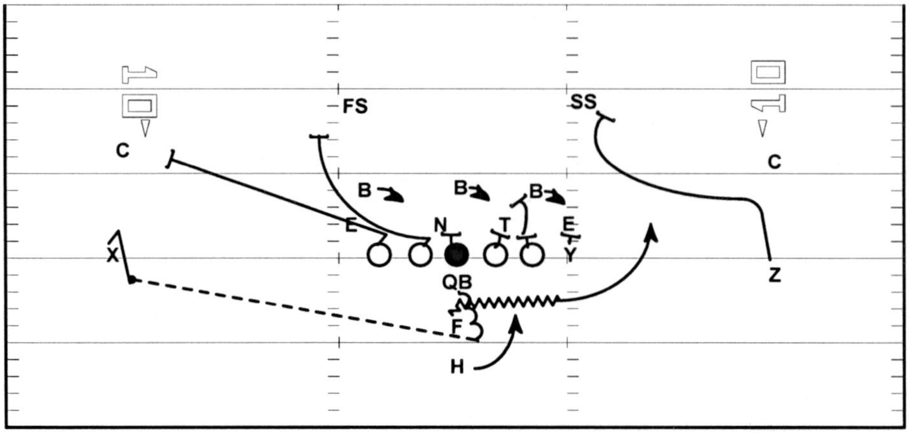

Description: This excellent screen play will get the ball into the playmaker's hands quickly. It is effective in run or pass down situations.

Assignments:

QB: Open and flash fakes inside zone right. Gains ground to the depth of three to four yards. Delivers the ball to X.

H: Executes inside zone right track.

F: Motions right and releases to block the edge pressure.

Y: Blocks inside zone right.

Z: Convoys to the near safety.

X: Jab steps. Comes back three steps. Secures quick screen pass.

LT: Slams. Releases and blocks the flat defender.

LG: Slams. Releases and blocks the alley.

C: Blocks inside zone right.

RG: Blocks inside zone right.

RT: Blocks inside zone right.

Coaching Points: The QB will flash zone right, then deliver the ball to X on a quick screen route. The screen receiver (X) should have a maximum split of 12 yards.

Play #2: Wide Receiver Screen Left—Ex. 1

Charlie Stubbs
University of Alabama

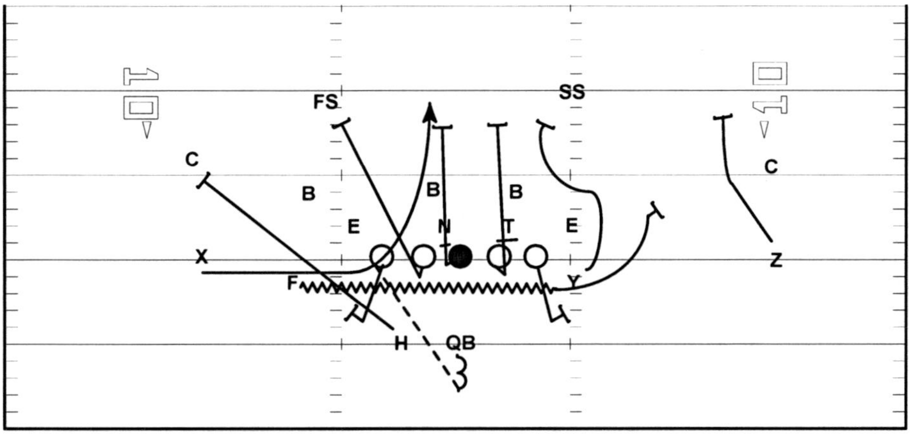

Description: This play is great versus an aggressive up-the-field pass rush. Wide receivers that have punt returning skills are best suited for this type of screen pass because they understand the wall blocking scheme and will show patience advancing the ball.

Assignments:

QB: Aligns in gun. Pumps right then delivers the ball to X on a wide receiver screen.

H: Free releases and blocks the most dangerous defender aligned on X (screen receiver).

F: Motions across. Blocks support defender inside out.

Y: Arc releases. Seals second level flow inside out.

Z: Blocks deep outside third area.

X: Executes tunnel screen (10 to 12 yard split).

LT: Executes dropback protection (five step).

LG: Slams for one count. Releases 45-degree angle left. Blocks most dangerous defender.

C: Slams for one count. Releases 45-degree angle left. Blocks most dangerous defender.

RG: Slams for one count. Releases 45-degree angle left. Blocks most dangerous defender.

RT: Executes dropback protection (five step).

Coaching Points: The screen receiver (X) must help find a passing lane between himself and the QB. The ball should be caught inside the offensive tackle's block.

Play #3: Wide Receiver Screen Left—Ex. 2

Charlie Stubbs
University of Alabama

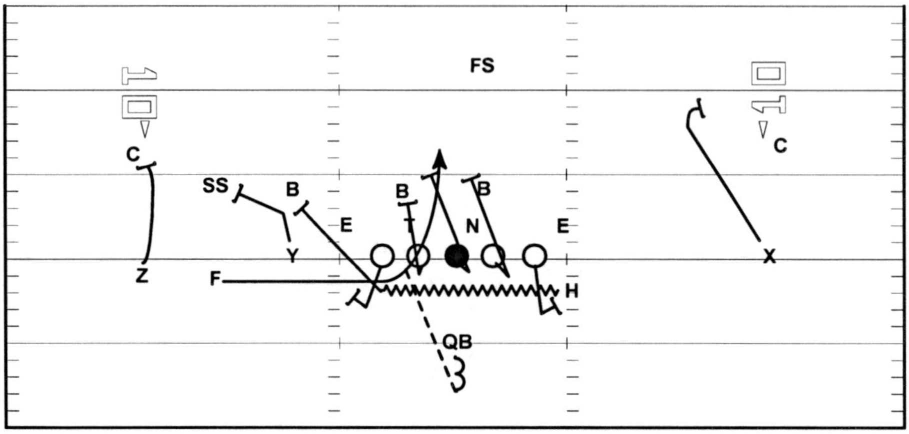

Description: This play is great versus an aggressive up-the-field pass rush. Wide receivers that have punt returning skills are best suited for this type of screen pass because they understand the wall blocking scheme and will show patience while advancing the ball.

Assignments:

QB: Aligns in gun and looks opposite the screen receiver. Then delivers the pass to F.

H: Motions across and blocks the most dangerous second-level defender aligned to F.

F: Executes tunnel screen (splits approximately 10 to 12 yards).

Y: Pushes and blocks defender inside out.

Z: Blocks man on.

X: Blocks man on inside out.

LT: Executes dropback protection (five step).

LG: Slams for one count and releases slightly left to block the most dangerous defender.

C: Slams for one count and releases slightly left to block the most dangerous defender.

RG: Slams for one count and releases slightly left to block the most dangerous defender.

RT: Executes dropback protection (five step).

Coaching Points: The screen receiver (F) must help find a passing lane for the QB. The ball should be caught inside the offensive tackle's block and behind the LOS.

Play #4: Double Pass Throwback Screen to Quarterback

Jeff Horton
University of Wisconsin

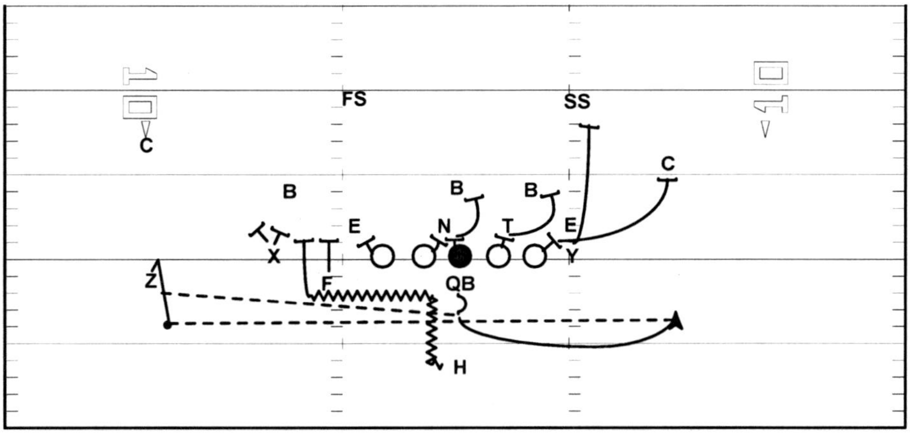

Description: Many defenses do not account for the QB as a potential screen receiver. This special play utilizes the skills of the flanker (Z) and the QB as playmakers.

Assignments:

QB: Aligns in gun and throws quick screen left to Z. Drifts away from screen five yards wider than the tight end's alignment.

H: Motions from backfield. Blocks most dangerous defender.

F: Blocks the most dangerous defender on the edge.

Y: Arc releases to the high safety.

Z: Executes a quick screen catch. Fakes run. Throws the ball to QB for screen.

X: Blocks most dangerous defender.

LT: Base blocks the defensive end.

LG: Combo blocks to second level.

C: Combo blocks to second level.

RG: Slams and releases to block the alley.

RT: Chips and releases to block the flat defender.

Coaching Points: The ball must be completed behind the LOS because offensive lineman will be down the field blocking.

Play #5: Sweep Right Screen Left to Tight End

Charlie Stubbs
Oregon State University

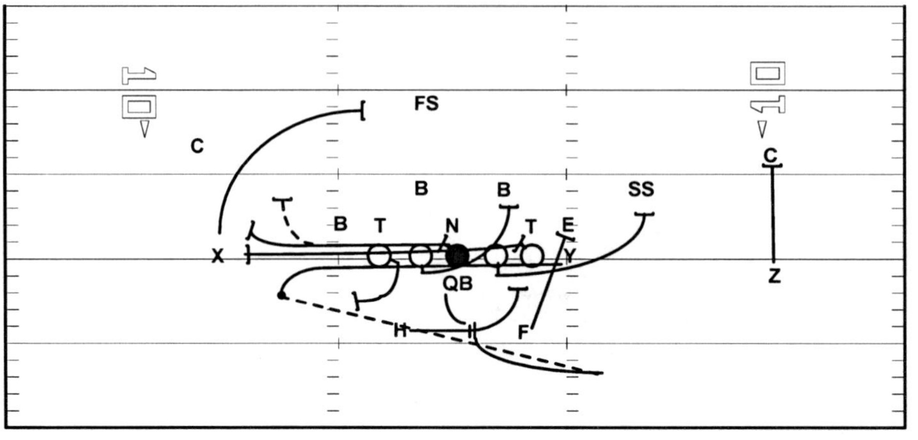

Description: In this fake sweep right, the tight end will block down following the playside offensive tackle. This play utilizes a two-man screen blocking scheme off of the full-flow sweep action.

Assignments:

QB: Reverses out and fakes sweep right. Rolls right and sets up five to seven yards behind the offensive tackle.

H: Executes sweep right track and runs downhill.

F: Executes sweep right block and cuts the end man on the LOS.

Y: Releases and blocks down following the playside tackle. Catches the screen pass on the weakside.

Z: Blocks man on.

X: Convoys to the near safety.

LT: Steps inside and arc releases to block backside flow.

LG: Pulls for sweep right blocking.

C: Slams and releases to block the flat defender or alley.

RG: Pulls for sweep right and blocks the support defender.

RT: Slams and releases to lead the tight end. Blocks the flat defender.

Coaching Points: The tight end must work his way through to find a passing lane for the QB. The ball must be completed behind the LOS.

Play #6: Fake Draw Right Crack Screen Left—Strong

Charlie Stubbs
Oregon State University

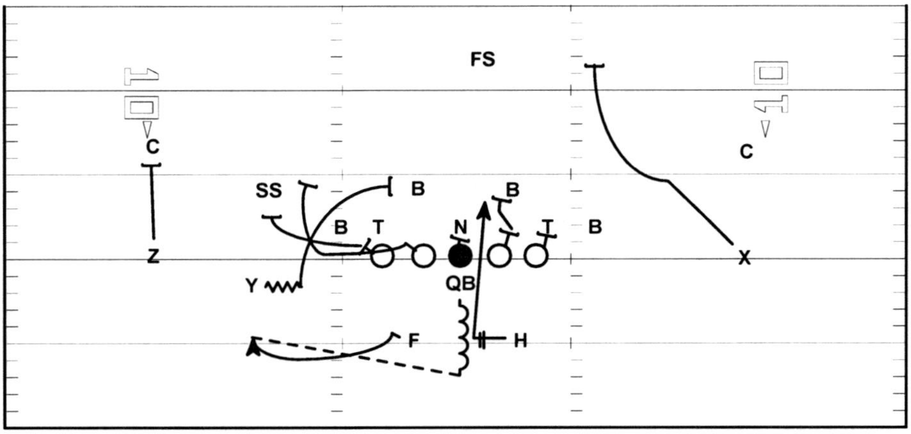

Description: This play is a screen pass off of the dropback passing game towards the strength of the formation. A great draw fake will occupy the defenders as the blockers are releasing to execute the blocking scheme.

Assignments:

QB: Open fakes draw right. Throws crack screen to F.

H: Executes draw right track with a great fake.

F: Pauses and bubbles for crack screen left.

Y: Motions inside and cracks the first defender inside off the LOS.

Z: Blocks man on.

X: Convoys to the near safety.

LT: Sets pass and releases to block the flat defender.

LG: Sets pass and releases to block the alley.

C: Base blocks.

RG: Base blocks.

RT: Base blocks.

Coaching Points: The QB must continue to gain ground after the draw fake. The ball must be completed behind the LOS because the offensive lineman will be blocking down the field.

Play #7: Fake Draw Right Crack Screen Left—Weak

Charlie Stubbs
Oregon State University

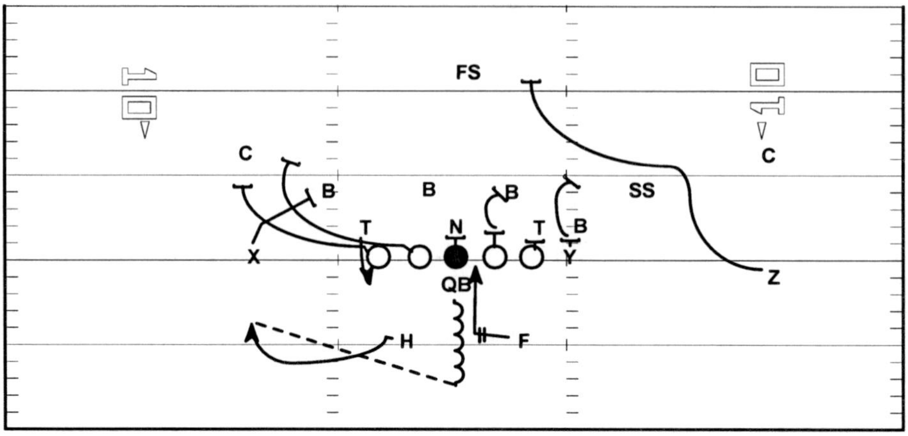

Description: This play is a screen pass off of the dropback passing game towards the weakness of the formation. A great draw fake will occupy the defenders as the blockers are releasing to execute the blocking scheme.

Assignments:

QB: Open fakes draw right. Throws crack screen to H.

H: Pauses and bubbles for the crack screen left.

F: Executes draw right track with a great fake.

Y: Slams and releases inside. Seals backside flow.

Z: Convoys to the middle safety.

X: Pushes and cracks the first defender inside off the LOS.

LT: Sets pass and releases to block the flat defender.

LG: Sets pass and releases to block the alley.

C: Base blocks.

RG: Base blocks.

RT: Base blocks.

Coaching Points: The QB must continue to gain ground after the draw fake. The ball must be completed behind the LOS because the offensive lineman will be blocking down the field.

Play #8: Zone Left Reverse Right Screen Left to Quarterback

Charlie Stubbs
University of Tulsa

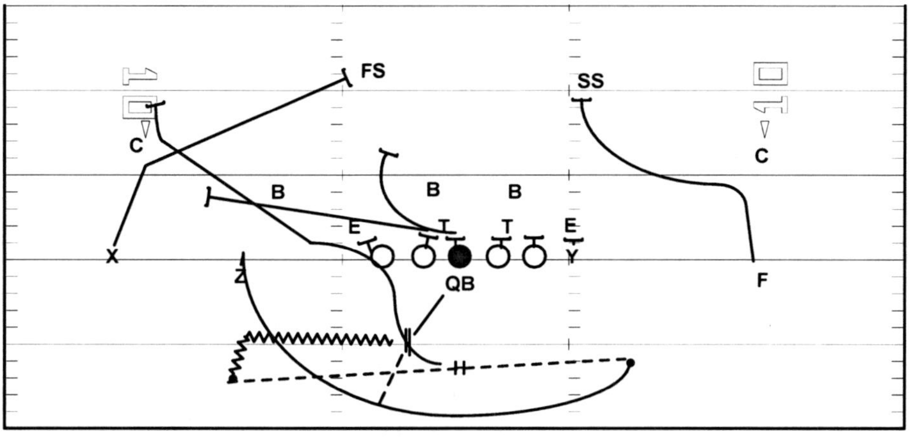

Description: This play offers a great opportunity to utilize two playmakers on a special play. Many defenses tend to neglect covering the QB as a potential receiver.

Assignments:

QB: Open fakes inside zone left. Pitches to Z on the reverse and drifts left to receive the screen pass.

H: Executes inside zone left track. Runs a wheel route and blocks the deep outside third area.

F: Convoy blocks to the near safety.

Y: Base blocks.

Z: Executes reverse track. Secures the pitch and sells the run. Sets up to throw screen pass to the QB.

X: Pushes and cracks the near safety.

LT: Base blocks the defensive end.

LG: Slams for two counts and releases to block the flat defender.

C: Slams for two counts and releases to block the alley.

RG: Base blocks.

RT: Base blocks.

Coaching Points: The reverse receiver (Z) must sell the run while gaining depth and then set up to execute the screen throw to the QB.

Play #9: Double Pass Screen to Quarterback

Robert Anae
Texas Tech University

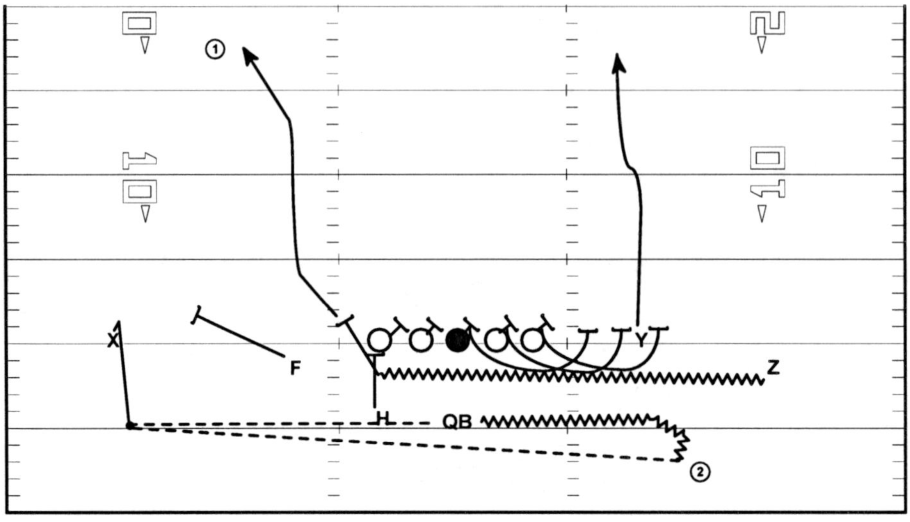

Description: This double pass has two options: a throw downfield to X or execution of a screen pass to the QB.

Assignments:

QB: Aligns in gun and throws the quick screen left to X. Drifts right for possible screen to QB.

H: Blocks edge pressure.

F: Releases horizontal to block the most dangerous defender behind the LOS.

Y: Executes best release on go route.

Z: Motions across and fakes block. Releases outside on a corner route.

X: Executes quick screen technique. Reads X to QB.

LT: Executes gap protection (rip).

LG: Executes gap protection (rip).

C: Executes gap protection (rip). Releases to screen.

RG: Executes gap protection (rip). Releases to screen.

RT: Executes gap protection (rip). Releases to screen.

Coaching Points: X has three potential reads: Z on a corner route, QB on the screen pass, or run the ball. The QB must make a go call if he receives the screen pass to let the offensive linemen know that they can release to block down the field.

Play #10: Sprint Right Screen Left to Fullback

Charlie Stubbs
University of Tulsa

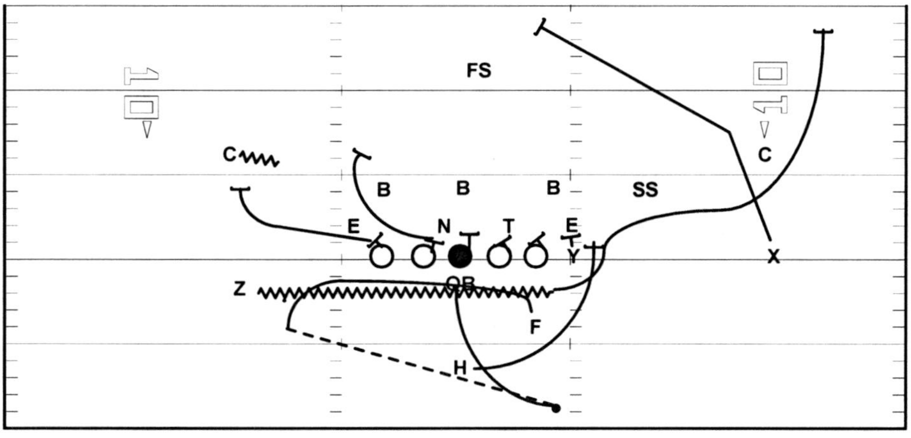

Description: This sprint out screen pass from an unbalanced formation is great versus flowing aggressive defenses.

Assignments:

QB: Opens and executes sprint right. Sets up for throwback screen pass to F.

H: Executes sprint right protection.

F: Steps up and releases left to catch the screen pass.

Y: Executes sprint right protection.

Z: Motions across and releases on the wheel route. Blocks the deep outside third area.

X: Executes a post route and blocks the deep middle area.

LT: Slams for two counts and releases to block the flat defender.

LG: Slams for two counts and releases to block the alley.

C: Executes sprint right protection.

RG: Executes sprint right protection.

RT: Executes sprint right protection.

Coaching Points: The QB must sell the sprint out action. F must hide and avoid contact as he is working to the weakside to receive the screen pass.

Play #11: Shift From Unbalanced Formation Double Screen Right

Charlie Stubbs
University of Louisville

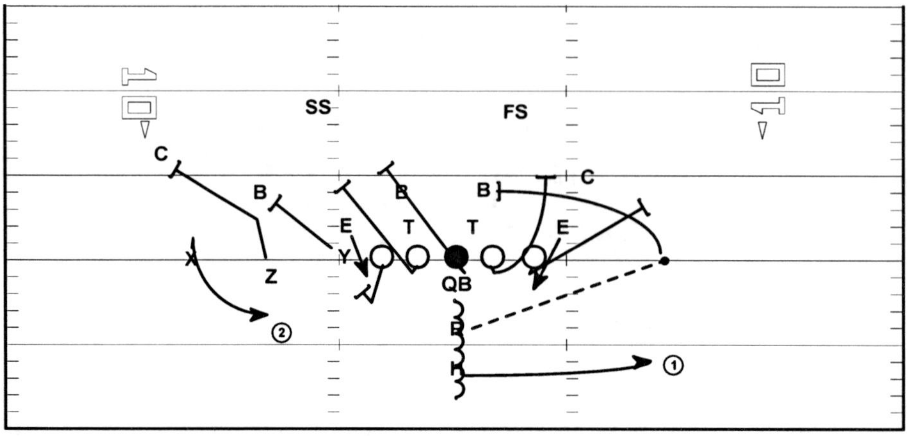

Description: This double screen special is great in run downs or short yardage situations.

Assignments:

QB: Drops back and reads H (swing screen) to X (tunnel screen).

H: Executes swing screen right.

R: Aligns in the I formation. Shifts to wide receiver alignment with a five-yard split. Blocks the first defender inside off of the LOS.

Y: Arc releases and blocks the support defender.

Z: Blocks the most dangerous defender aligned on X.

X: Executes tunnel screen (jab steps and arcs to depth of four yards).

LT: Executes dropback protection with a drop and cut of the defensive end.

LG: Slams and releases left at a 45-degree angle. Blocks the most dangerous defender.

C: Slams and releases left at a 45-degree angle. Blocks the most dangerous defender.

RG: Slams and releases to block the alley.

RT: Sets pass and releases to block the flat defender.

Coaching Points: The fullback (R) will shift on the QB command. The QB can throw the swing screen to the back, or if the defenders peel off, he can progress to the tunnel screen on the backside.

Play #12: Double Screen Right With Back Motion

Charlie Stubbs
University of Tulsa

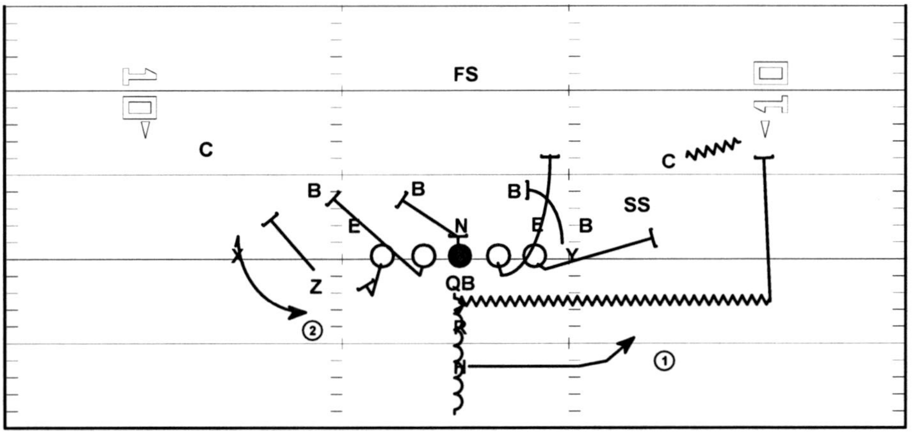

Description: This variation of the double screen is excellent on first down situations.

Assignments:

QB: Drops back and reads H (swing screen) to X (tunnel screen).

H: Executes swing screen right.

R: Motions wide and blocks the deep secondary defender. Does not block support defender.

Y: Executes best release and blocks the first defender inside off of the LOS.

Z: Blocks the most dangerous defender aligned on X.

X: Executes tunnel screen (jab steps and arcs to depth of four yards).

LT: Executes dropback protection with a drop and cut of the defensive end.

LG: Slams and releases left at a 45-degree angle. Blocks the most dangerous defender.

C: Slams and releases left at a 45-degree angle. Blocks the most dangerous defender.

RG: Slams and releases to block the alley.

RT: Sets pass and releases to block the flat defender.

Coaching Points: The QB can either throw the swing screen to the back, or if the defenders peel, he can progress to tunnel screen on the backside.

Play #13: Double Screen Right With Hip Motion

Charlie Stubbs
University of Central Missouri

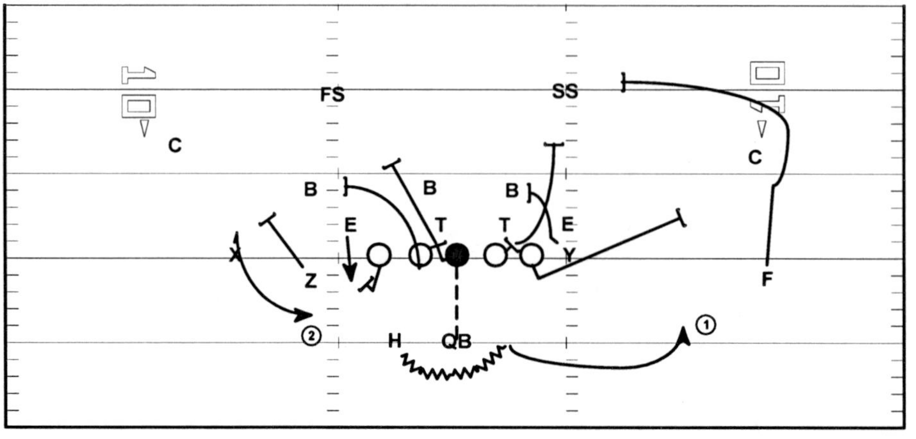

Description: The double screen with hip (short back) motion is excellent on passing downs from the gun alignment.

Assignments:

QB: Aligns in gun and reads H (swing screen) to X (tunnel screen).

H: Executes hip motion (short motion to opposite side of QB). Pauses and executes the swing screen right.

F: Blocks the deep third or half safety. Does not block support defender.

Y: Executes the best release and blocks the first defender inside off of the LOS.

Z: Blocks the most dangerous defender aligned on X.

X: Executes tunnel screen (jab steps and arcs to depth of four yards).

LT: Executes dropback protection with a drop and cut of the defensive end.

LG: Slams and releases left at a 45-degree angle. Blocks the most dangerous defender.

C: Slams and releases left at a 45-degree angle. Blocks the most dangerous defender.

RG: Slams and releases to block the alley.

RT: Sets pass and releases to block the flat defender.

Coaching Points: The QB is aligned in gun, and on the snap, he must keep eyes straight ahead. H should pause before releasing on the swing screen. This delay will tempt the defensive end to rush the passer. The QB will either throw the swing pass to the back, or if the defenders peel off, the QB will progress to the tunnel screen on the backside.

Play #14: Fake Bubble Left Slip Screen Right

Charlie Stubbs
University of Tulsa

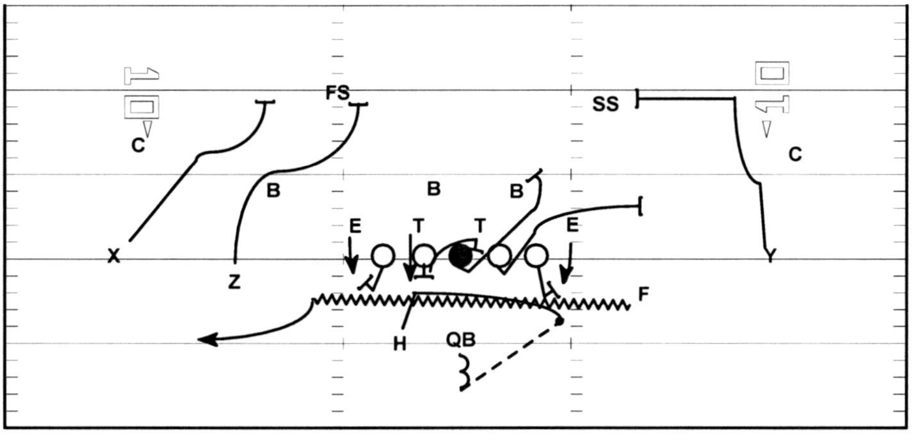

Description: This play is a basic one-count screen which is excellent versus zone, man, or blitzing defenses.

Assignments:

QB: Aligns in gun and fakes the bubble left. Executes slip screen pass right to H.

H: Aligns opposite the screen direction and crosses underneath. Secures the slip screen pass.

F: Motions across and fakes the catch with the bubble action.

Y: Releases outside and executes a wrap around route (12 to 14 yards). Blocks the near safety.

Z: Convoy blocks to the near safety.

X: Convoy blocks to the near safety.

LT: Executes dropback protection.

LG: Slams for one count and releases to peel back for defenders in pursuit from behind.

C: Slams for one count and releases to block the alley. In man coverage, must be prepared to block the linebacker covering H.

RG: Slams for one count and releases to block the flat defender.

RT: Executes dropback protection.

Coaching Points: The QB will fake a bubble pass to F to occupy the defenders' eyes. H (screen back) must be prepared to receive the ball quickly versus blitz situations while on the run.

Play #15: Fake F Drag Slip Screen Left

Charlie Stubbs
University of Tulsa

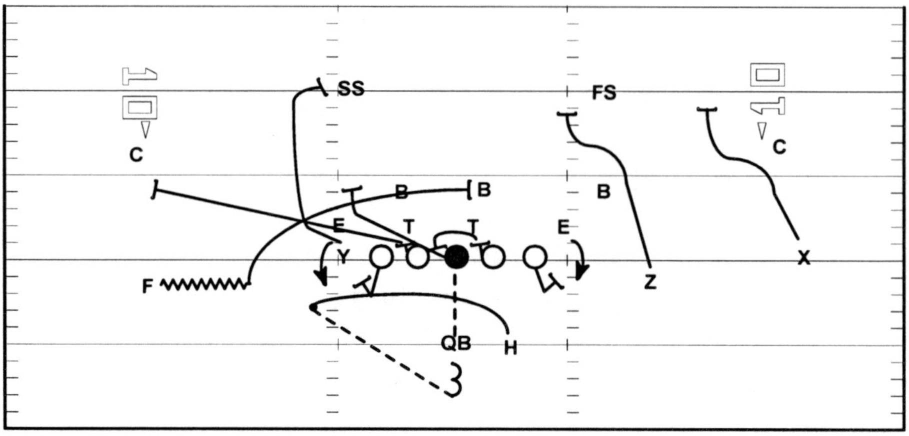

Description: This play is a basic one-count screen which is excellent versus zone, man, or blitzing defenses.

Assignments:

QB: Aligns in gun and fakes the F drag. Executes slip screen pass left to H.

H: Aligns opposite screen direction and crosses underneath. Secures slip screen pass.

F: Motions inside and executes a drag route underneath Y. Blocks the backside inside linebacker.

Y: Executes the best release and runs a wrap around route (12 to 14 yards). Blocks the high safety.

Z: Releases outside to the near safety.

X: Convoy blocks.

LT: Executes dropback protection.

LG: Slams for one count and releases to block the flat defender.

C: Slams for one count and releases to block the alley. Man coverage must be prepared to block the linebacker covering H.

RG: Slams for one count and releases to peel back for defenders in pursuit from behind.

RT: Executes dropback protection.

Coaching Points: The QB will focus on F with the drag route. The screen back (H) must be prepared to receive the ball quickly versus blitz situations while on the run.

Play #16: Pre-Snap Movement Slip Screen Left

Charlie Stubbs
University of Tulsa

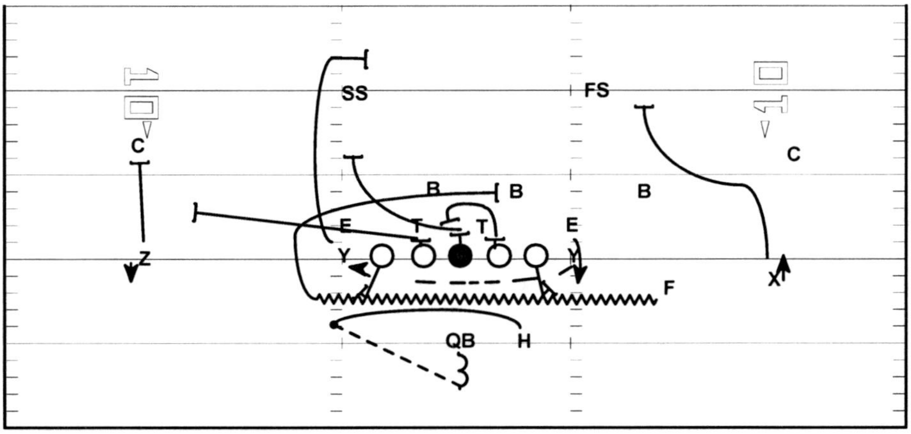

Description: The pre-snap movement will cause defensive confusion or hesitation and makes this play a great call versus zone, man, or blitz coverage.

Assignments:

QB: Aligns in gun and fakes the F drag route. Executes slip screen pass left to H.

H: Aligns opposite the screen direction and crosses underneath. Secures the slip screen pass.

F: Motions across and executes a drag route underneath Y. Blocks the backside inside linebacker.

Y: Executes the best release and runs a wrap around route (12 to 14 yards). Blocks the high safety.

Z: Blocks man on.

X: Convoy blocks to the near safety.

LT: Executes dropback protection.

LG: Slams for one count and releases to block the flat defender.

C: Slams for one count and releases to block the alley. Man coverage must be prepared to block the linebacker covering H.

RG: Slams for one count and releases to peel back for defenders in pursuit from behind.

RT: Executes dropback protection.

Coaching Points: The QB will focus on F with the drag route. The screen back (H) must be prepared to receive the ball quickly versus blitz situations while on the run.

Play #17: Sprint Right Throwback Screen Left

Charlie Stubbs
University of Central Missouri

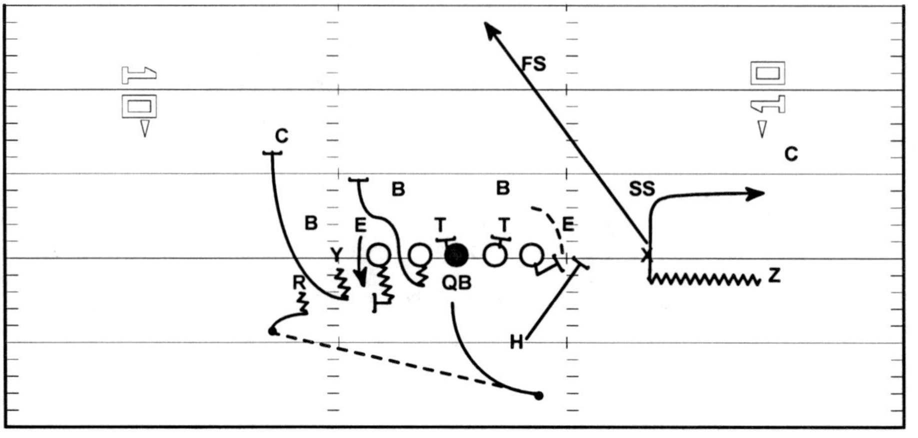

Description: The sprint out throwback screen to R (or fullback) offers misdirection to confuse the defense.

Assignments:

QB: Opens and sprints right. Sets up for throwback screen to R. Z is the hot receiver versus pressure and blitz situations.

H: Executes sprint right protection and blocks the edge.

R: Executes hinge protection and sets up for the throwback screen.

Y: Hinges and arc releases to block the outside third defender.

Z: Motions short inside behind X. Executes a speed break out (depth five yards). Hot WR versus blitz.

X: Runs a diagonal route to the middle of the field.

LT: Executes sprint right protection and hinges. Cut blocks the defensive end.

LG: Executes sprint right protection and hinges. Releases to block the alley.

C: Blocks man on.

RG: Blocks man on.

RT: Executes sprint right protection.

Coaching Points: The QB has two possible reads. Versus zone coverage, he will look to R on the throwback screen. Versus pressure/blitz (man coverage), he will execute the hot throw to Z.

Play #18: Rub Screen Right R Go

Charlie Stubbs
University of Central Missouri

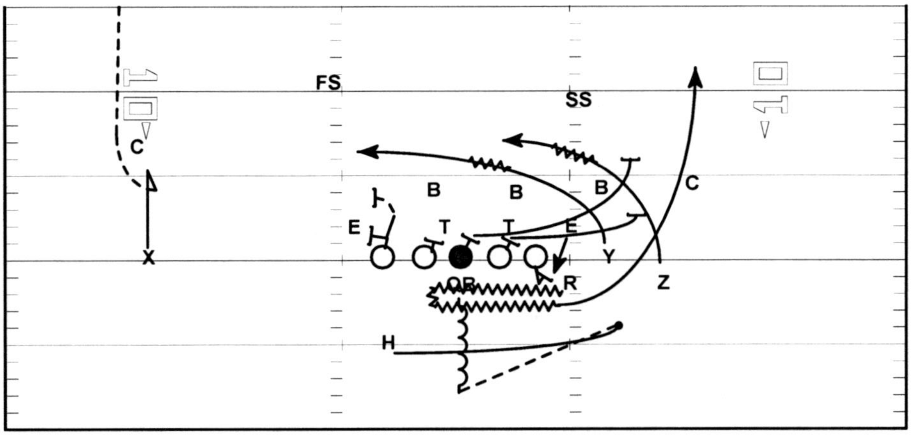

Description: This is an excellent screen pass versus man coverage with lots of rubs from the bunch alignment.

Assignments:

QB: Drops back and reads the rub screen right with a possible hot receiver (X) on a hitch route.

H: Aligns left and executes a swing right for the screen pass.

R: Executes return motion then arc releases on a go route.

Y: Executes a drag route (four to six yards) looking for a rub.

Z: Executes a cross route (six to eight yards) looking for a rub.

X: Executes a hitch route (five yards). Possible hot receiver.

LT: Executes sprint right protection.

LG: Executes sprint right protection.

C: Executes sprint right protection and releases to block the alley with a one count release.

RG: Executes sprint right protection and releases to block the flat defender with a one count release.

RT: Executes sprint right protection.

Coaching Points: The QB must key R on the go route to ensure that the corner or safety gets depth as he executes the screen pass. The QB must throw the hitch route (X) on backside versus edge pressure playside.

Play #19: Fun Pass

Charlie Stubbs
University of Alabama

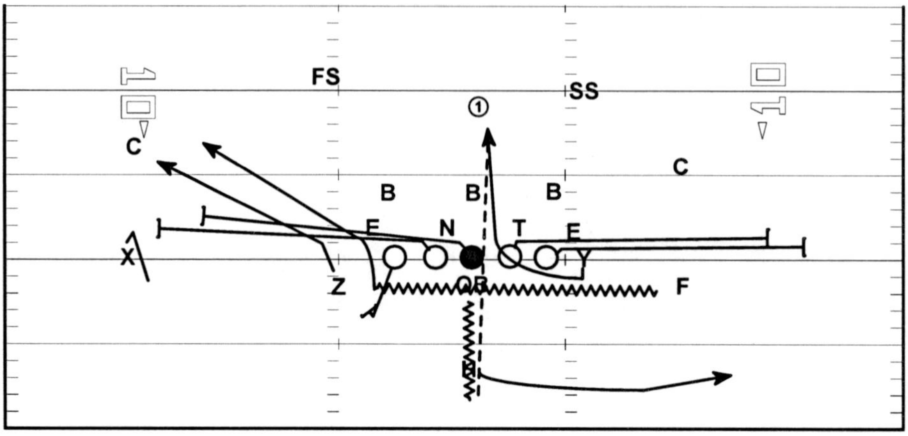

Description: This pass complements the double screen package. It is a great play versus defenses that key on the OL quickly for tips on screens (vacating the middle of the field).

Assignments:

QB: Drops quickly. Pump fakes WR screen to left or looks at swing route by H. Gains ground. Delivers ball to Y.

H: Executes swing screen route (flash hands).

F: Executes fly motion. Fakes screen block. Cannot make contact downfield.

Y: Drop steps. Loses one to two yards. Executes route through the A gap. Receives the ball approximately five to seven yards downfield.

Z: Fakes screen block. Cannot make contact downfield.

X: Fakes screen. Simulates making catch.

LT: Executes five-step pass protection.

LG: Slams. Releases down the LOS (left).

C: Slams. Releases down the LOS (left).

RG: Slams. Releases down the LOS (right).

RT: Slams. Releases down the LOS (right).

Coaching Points: The QB may execute a pump fake to H first, and then locate Y. This play complements the basic double screen package. Reminder: The OL cannot be downfield because the pass will be completed beyond the LOS.

Play #20: Fake Wide Receiver Screen Special—Ex. 1

Charlie Stubbs
University of Alabama

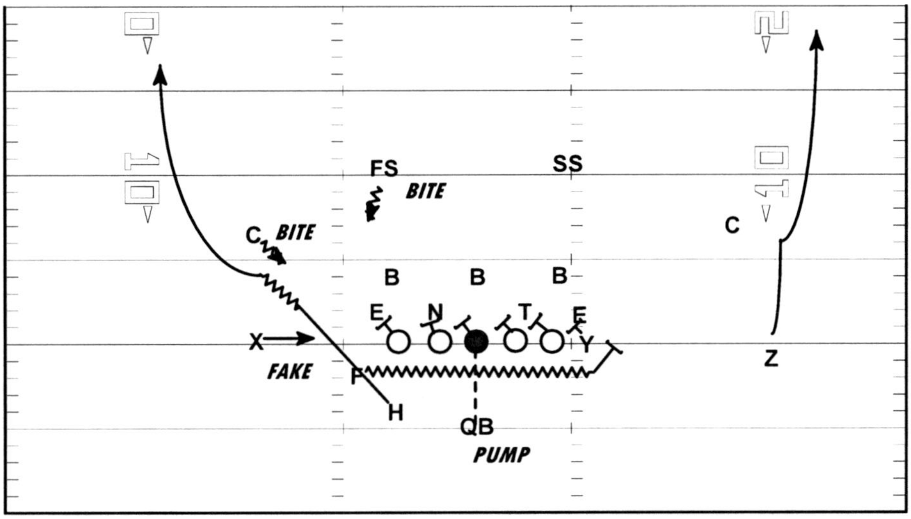

Description: This play is a great way to offset an aggressive defense attacking the wide receiver screen package.

Assignments:

QB: Utilizes gun alignment. Pump fakes WR screen left. Then keys H on route.

H: Aligns five yards deep behind weakside OT. Fake blocks for X (screen) WR. Executes wheel route.

F: Executes fly motion. Protects D gap.

Y: Liz (gap protection).

Z: Runs a go route.

X: Fakes screen (flash hands).

LT: Liz (gap protection).

LG: Liz (gap protection).

C: Liz (gap protection).

RG: Liz (gap protection).

RT: Liz (gap protection).

Coaching Points: The QB must execute a pump fake on screen. The primary target is H on the wheel route.

Play #21: Fake Wide Receiver Screen Special—Ex. 2

Charlie Stubbs
University of Alabama

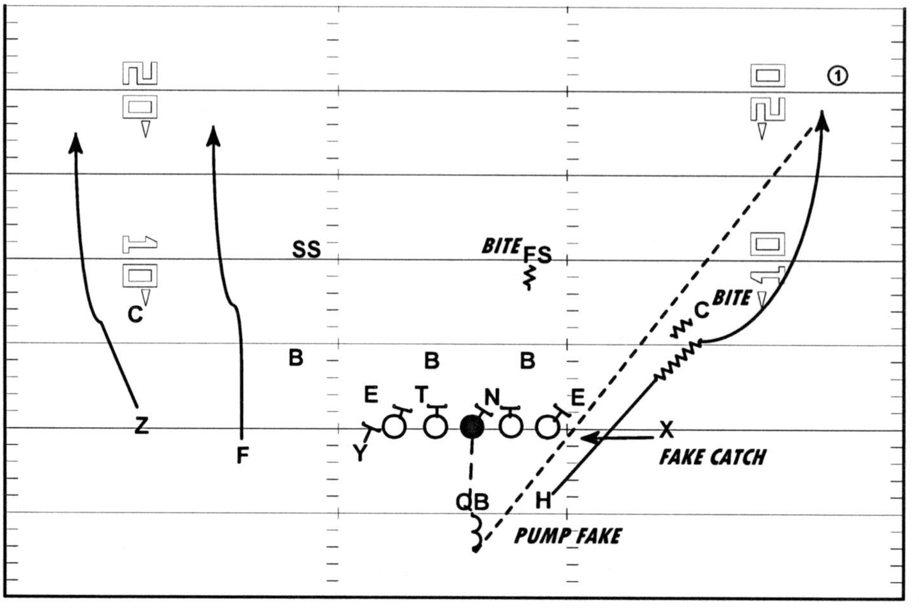

Description: This play complements the WR screen package. It is a great play versus an aggressive defense.

Assignments:

QB: Aligns in gun.

H: Aligns behind the OT (five-yard depth). Fakes block on support. Executes wheel route.

F: Releases outside on go route.

Y: Checks protection. Helps.

Z: Releases outside on go route.

X: Fakes catch on WR screen.

LT: Executes dropback protection (five step).

LG: Executes dropback protection (five step).

C: Executes dropback protection (five step).

RG: Executes dropback protection (five step).

RT: Executes dropback protection (five step).

Coaching Points: The QB will pump fake to X on a screen route then progress to H on a wheel route.

Play #22: Flash Double Arc

Charlie Stubbs
University of Central Missouri

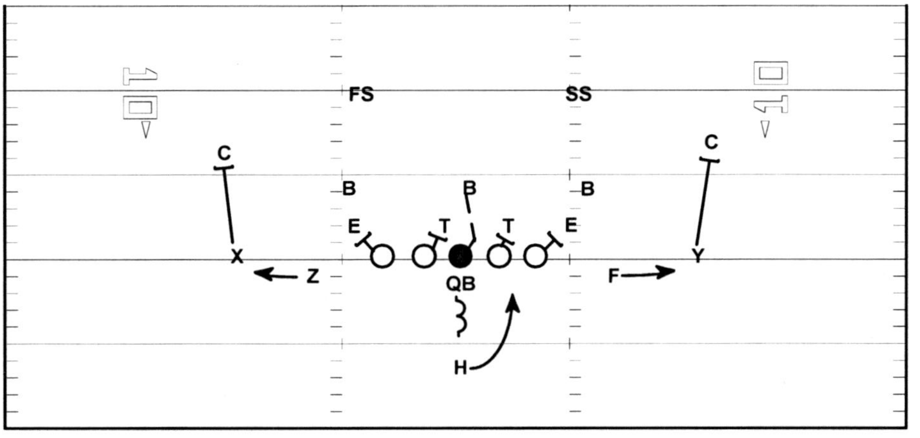

Description: This quick hitting pass to either inside receiver has the intent to out leverage the defense that is not displaced.

Assignments:

QB: Drop steps. Executes quick throw.

H: Executes inside zone track.

F: Executes arc route.

Y: Blocks man over.

Z: Executes arc route.

X: Blocks man over.

LT: Cuts down lineman.

LG: Executes aggressive solid protection.

C: Executes aggressive solid protection.

RG: Executes aggressive solid protection.

RT: Cuts down lineman.

Coaching Points: The QB must pick a side and key the alignment of outside linebackers (uncovered inside receivers rule).

Play #23: Shovel Pass Right

Charlie Stubbs
University of Alabama

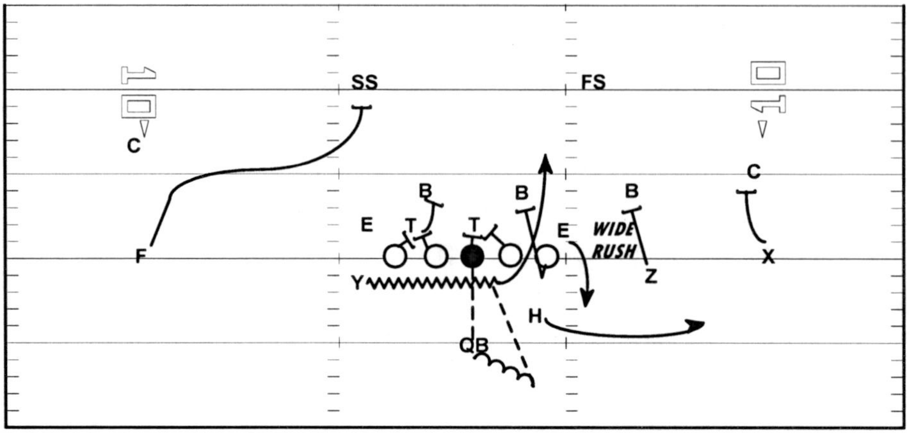

Description: This shovel pass play complements the dropback passing game versus a wide pass rush.

Assignments:

QB: Aligns in gun. Keys defensive end.

H: Aligns wide. Executes speed option right from gun alignment.

F: Convoys to near safety.

Y: Aligns off LOS. Releases horizontal for shovel pass phase.

Z: Blocks man on.

X: Blocks man on.

LT: Blocks inside zone right rules.

LG: Blocks inside zone right rules.

C: Blocks inside zone right rules.

RG: Blocks inside zone right rules.

RT: Sets with pass protection technique; invites DE up the field. Blocks first linebacker inside.

Coaching Points: The QB must read the DE or edge rusher. For a wide rush, he executes the shovel pass; for a tight rush, he executes the speed option phase.

Play #24: Shovel Pass Left

Charlie Stubbs
University of Nevada Las Vegas

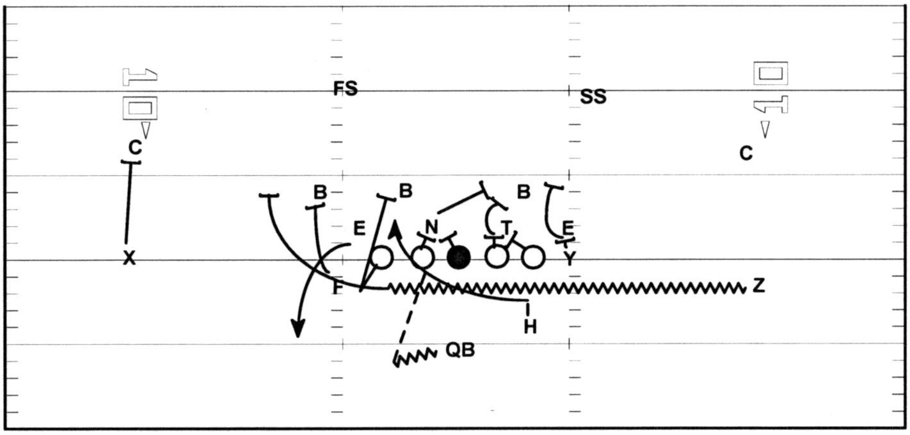

Description: A great play versus an aggressive wide pass rush.

Assignments:

QB: Aligns in gun. Drifts left. Reads DE (executes shovel pass).

H: Aligns on right side of QB. Executes track to receive shovel pass.

F: Blocks most dangerous defender.

Y: Executes inside zone left blocking scheme.

Z: Motions across. Releases and blocks most dangerous defender.

X: Blocks most dangerous defender.

LT: Sets with pass protection technique (invites DE up the field). Blocks first linebacker inside.

LG: Executes double-team. Great movement.

C: Executes double-team. Great movement.

RG: Executes combo block with the tackle.

RT: Executes combo block with the guard.

Coaching Points: The QB must show pass while inviting the DE upfield. The shovel pass is to H.

Play #25: Shovel Pass With Lead Blocker

Charlie Stubbs
University of Central Missouri

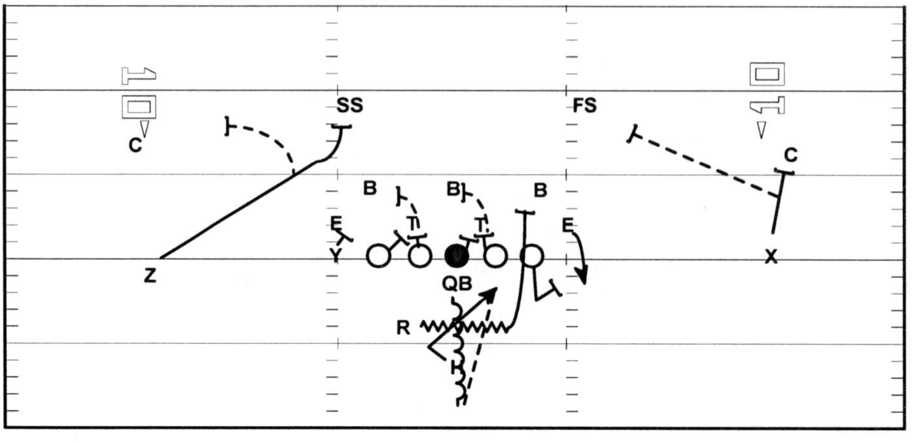

Description: The shovel pass concept is used in this deceptive pass play. R is the lead blocker. This play is effective versus an upfield wide rush by the defensive end.

Assignments:

QB: Drops back (sells pass). Gains a depth of seven to nine yards.

H: Moves two steps left. Then angles and receives the shovel pass.

R: Motions (short). Blocks first linebacker inside (playside).

Y: Executes PAP protection—zone (inside gap).

Z: Releases inside and blocks the near safety.

X: Blocks most dangerous man to the near safety.

LT: Executes aggressive zone blocking to second level.

LG: Executes aggressive zone blocking to second level.

C: Executes aggressive zone blocking to second level.

RG: Executes aggressive zone blocking to second level.

RT: Executes dropback protection. Invites the defensive end up the field.

Coaching Points: The QB must sell the dropback pass. H must be patient.

3

Fake Draw Passes

Doug Benc/Getty Images

Play #26: Fake Draw Right All Takeoff (Four Vertical)—Ex. 1

Charlie Stubbs
University of Tulsa

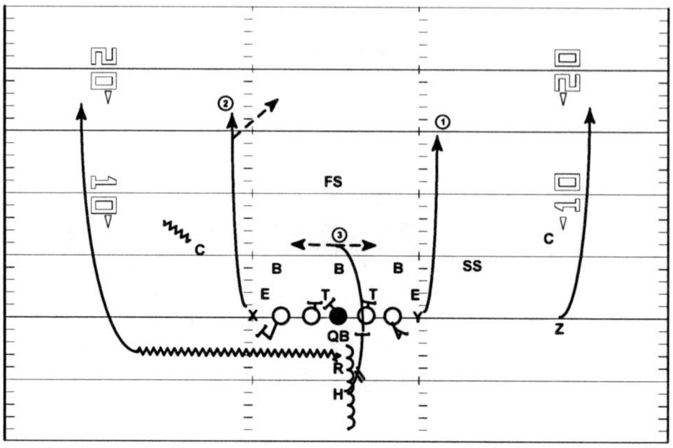

Description: This four vertical concept play has back motion to build a 2x2 alignment. Spacing and landmarks for the receivers are very important. This play is excellent versus cover 3 and is best executed from the middle of the field.

Assignments:

QB: Drops back (five step) and executes fake draw right. Sets up approximately six to seven yards deep.

H: Executes draw right (great fake). Checks protection (double read). Releases on option route (six-yard depth). Versus dog/blitz disregards fake and must block protection responsibility.

R: Motions to wide alignment. Runs a takeoff route (landmark is the base of the numbers).

Y: Arc releases on a takeoff route (landmark is the hash mark).

Z: Executes a takeoff route (landmark is the base of the numbers).

X: Arc releases on a takeoff route (landmark is the hash mark). Runs a bender (18- to 20-yard depth) versus cover 2.

LT: Executes drop back protection (five step).

LG: Executes drop back protection (five step).

C: Executes drop back protection (five step).

RG: Executes drop back protection (five step).

RT: Executes drop back protection (five step).

Coaching Points: The QB progression versus a single high safety is read Y to X to H. The QB must key the free safety (look the FS off). The QB progression versus two high safeties is Y to X (bender) to H.

Play #27: Fake Draw Right All Takeoff (Four Vertical)—Ex. 2

Charlie Stubbs
University of Tulsa/University of Central Missouri

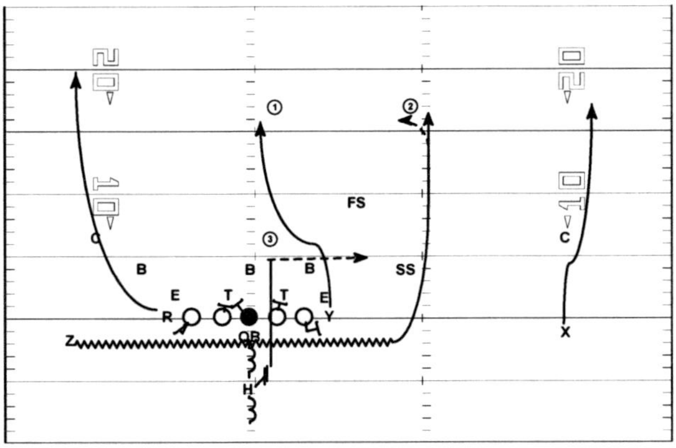

Description: This four vertical concept has wide receiver motion to build a 3x1 alignment. Spacing and landmarks are very important for the receivers. This play is excellent versus a single high safety and is best executed from the hash.

Assignments:

QB: Drops back (five step) and executes fake draw right. Sets up approximately six to seven yards deep.

H: Executes draw right (great fake). Checks protection (double read). Releases on option route (six-yard depth). Versus dog/blitz disregards fake and must block protection responsibility.

R: Arc releases on a takeoff route (landmark is the base of the numbers).

Y: Best releases. Climbs to far hash on a takeoff route (landmark is the hash mark). Does not cross the hash.

Z: Motions across. Releases on a takeoff route (landmark is the hash mark). Runs a bender (18- to 20-yard depth) versus cover 2.

X: Executes a takeoff route (landmark is the base of the numbers).

LT: Executes drop back protection (five step).

LG: Executes drop back protection (five step).

C: Executes drop back protection (five step).

RG: Executes drop back protection (five step).

RT: Executes drop back protection (five step).

Coaching Points: The QB progression versus a single high safety is read Y to Z to H. QB must key the free safety (look the FS off). Versus two high safeties the read is Y to Z (bender) to H.

Play #28: Fake Draw Right All Takeoff (Four Vertical)—Ex. 3

Charlie Stubbs
University of Tulsa

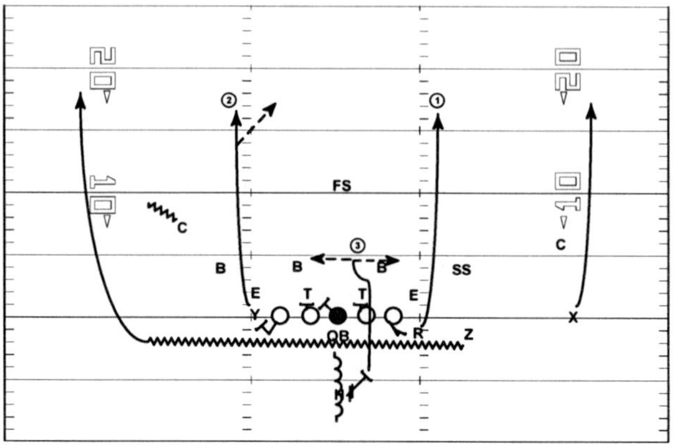

Description: This pass play has four vertical routes with a draw fake. Spacing and landmarks for the receivers are very important. This play is excellent versus cover 3 and is best executed from the middle of the field.

Assignments:

QB: Drops back (five step) and executes fake draw right. Sets up approximately six to seven yards deep.

H: Executes draw right (great fake). Checks protection (double read). Releases on option route (six-yard depth). Versus dog/blitz disregards fake and must block protection responsibility.

R: Arc releases on a takeoff route (landmark is the hash mark).

Y: Arc releases on a takeoff route (landmark is the hash mark). Runs a bender (18- to 20-yard depth) versus cover 2.

Z: Motions across to wide alignment. Runs a takeoff route (landmark is the base of the numbers).

X: Executes a takeoff route (landmark is the base of the numbers).

LT: Executes drop back protection (five step).

LG: Executes drop back protection (five step).

C: Executes drop back protection (five step).

RG: Executes drop back protection (five step).

RT: Executes drop back protection (five step).

Coaching Points: The QB progression versus a single high safety is read R to Y to H. The QB must key the free safety (look the FS off). The QB progression versus two high safeties is R to Y (bender) to H.

Play #29: Fake Draw Right Backs Cross

Charlie Stubbs
University of Alabama

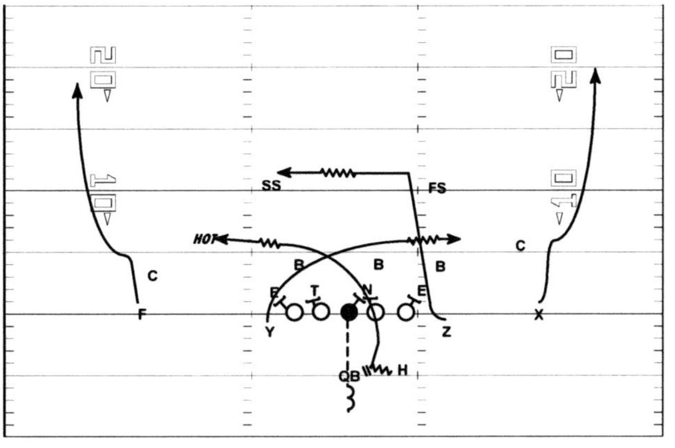

Description: This play is a pass play (to a playmaker) which exploits underneath coverage. After a draw fake, defenses have a tendency to disregard the back when they realize he doesn't have the ball.

Assignments:

QB: Aligns in gun. Fakes draw to H.

H: Fakes draw. Releases into route, crossing underneath Y. Responsible for mesh (rub).

F: Releases outside on go route.

Y: Checks release on drag route. Responsible for depth of route (four to six yards).

Z: Runs a wrap around route (12 to 14 yards).

X: Releases outside on a go route.

LT: Executes dropback protection (five step).

LG: Executes dropback protection (five step).

C: Executes dropback protection (five step).

RG: Executes dropback protection (five step).

RT: Executes dropback protection (five step).

Coaching Points: QB fakes a draw to H then reads Z (wrap around) to H on crossing route after mesh. H is the hot receiver.

4

Reverses, Reverse Passes, and Fake Reverse Passes

University of Alabama Sports Information Department

Play #30: Counter Right Reverse Left–Weak

Charlie Stubbs
University of Tulsa

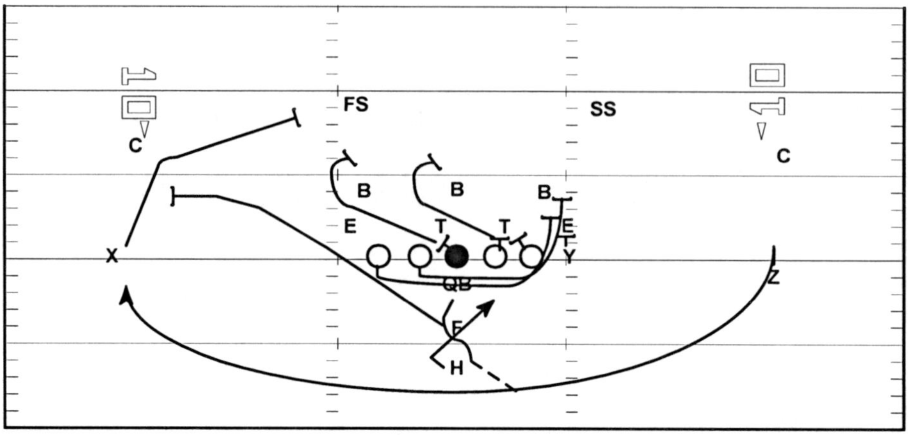

Description: This misdirection play reverses off of the counter action.

Assignments:

QB: Reverses out. Fakes counter. Tosses the ball to Z.

H: Executes counter right track (great fake).

F: Executes counter blocking release. Blocks the support defender in the flat area.

Y: Base blocks the defensive end.

Z: Executes the reverse track. Gets depth. Secures the toss.

X: Pushes and cracks the near safety.

LT: Blocks counter right rules.

LG: Blocks counter right rules.

C: Blocks left. Releases to seal area for reverse.

RG: Blocks counter right rules. Releases to seal area for reverse.

RT: Blocks counter right rules.

Coaching Points: QB will toss the ball to Z on the reverse. This action forces Z to get depth.

Play #31: Counter Right Reverse Left–Strong

Charlie Stubbs
University of Nevada Las Vegas

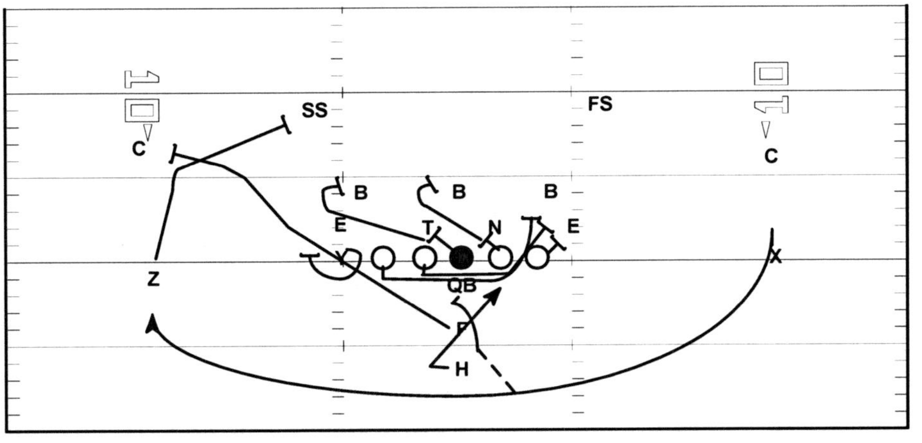

Description: This great reverse play complements the basic counter blocking scheme.

Assignments:

QB: Reverses out. Fakes counter. Tosses the ball to X.

H: Executes counter right track (great fake).

F: Executes counter blocking release. Provides block support (flat area).

Y: Steps inside. Executes circle to block the end man on the LOS.

Z: Pushes and cracks the near safety.

X: Executes the reverse track. Gets depth. Secures the toss.

LT: Blocks counter right rules.

LG: Blocks counter right rules.

C: Blocks left. Releases to seal area for reverse.

RG: Blocks counter right rules. Releases to seal area for reverse.

RT: Blocks counter right rules.

Coaching Points: The QB will toss the ball to X on the reverse. This action forces X to get depth.

Play #32: Toss Right Reverse Left

Charlie Stubbs
University of Alabama

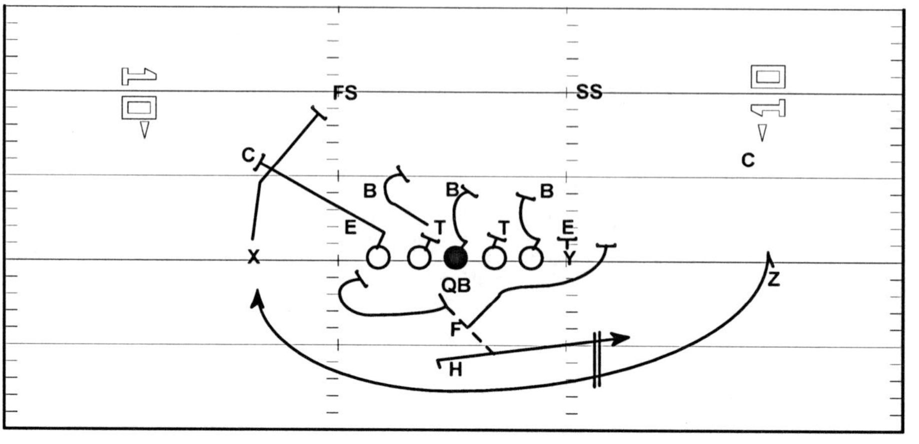

Description: The misdirection in this play comes from a reverse off of the toss action.

Assignments:

QB: Reverses out. Executes toss. Assists with protection on backside flow.

H: Executes toss track. Secures ball (sells run). Hands the ball off to Z.

F: Executes toss track. Blocks the support defender.

Y: Executes toss blocking scheme.

Z: Executes reverse track. Secures handoff. Gets depth.

X: Pushes and cracks the near safety.

LT: Steps to inside gap. Releases flat to block the support defender.

LG: Slams near defensive lineman. Releases to block second level pursuit.

C: Zone blocks to second level.

RG: Zone blocks to second level.

RT: Zone blocks to second level.

Coaching Points: Reverse wide receiver (Z) should have maximum split (12 to 14 yards) so that H can sell the run to get the defense to flow.

Play #33: Zone Right Reverse Left—Ex. 1

Charlie Stubbs
University of Alabama

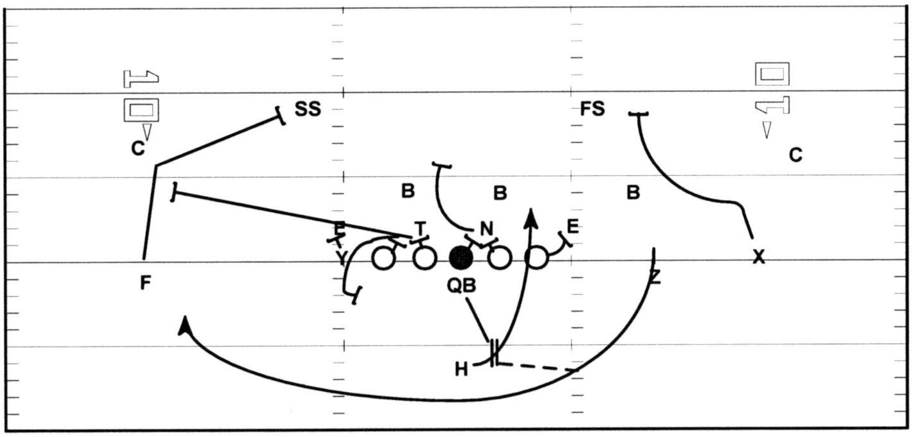

Description: The misdirection in this play comes from the reverse off of the inside zone action.

Assignments:

QB: Open fakes inside zone right. Pitches the ball to Z on the reverse.

H: Executes inside zone right track (great fake).

F: Pushes and cracks the near safety.

Y: Base blocks the man over.

Z: Executes the reverse track. Gets depth. Receives pitch.

X: Convoy blocks to the near safety.

LT: Slams inside gap. Circles to block defensive flow.

LG: Slams defensive lineman. Releases to block the flat defender.

C: Combo blocks the second level.

RG: Combo blocks the second level.

RT: Base blocks the man over.

Coaching Points: Reverse receiver (Z) must get depth to receive the pitch. This action will help him avoid any backside flow.

Play #34: Zone Right Reverse Left—Ex. 2

Charlie Stubbs
University of Tulsa

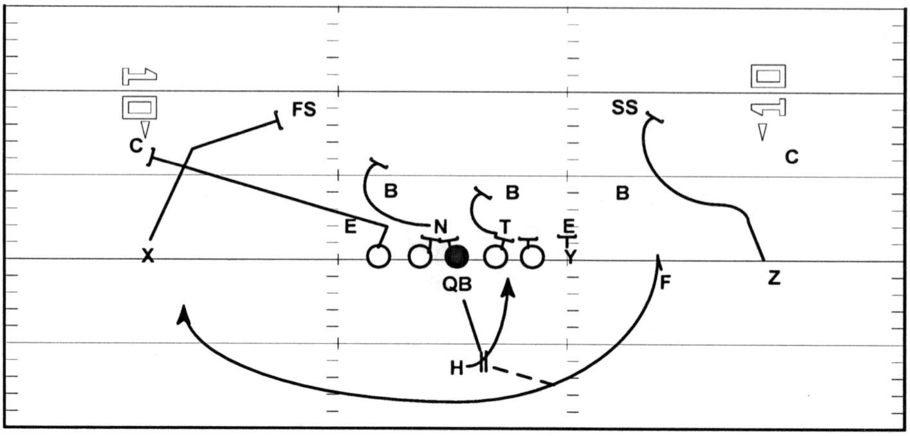

Description: The misdirection in this play comes from the reverse off of the inside zone action.

Assignments:

QB: Open fakes inside zone right. Pitches the ball to F on the reverse.

H: Executes inside zone right track (great fake).

F: Executes the reverse track. Gets depth. Receives pitch.

Y: Base blocks the man over.

Z: Convoy blocks to the near safety.

X: Pushes and cracks the near safety.

LT: Steps to inside gap. Releases to block the flat defender.

LG: Slams inside. Releases to block second level flow.

C: Zone blocks.

RG: Combo blocks to the second level.

RT: Combo blocks to the second level.

Coaching Points: The reverse receiver (F) must get depth to receive the pitch. This action will help him avoid any backside flow.

Play #35: Speed Option Right Reverse Left

Charlie Stubbs
University of Tulsa

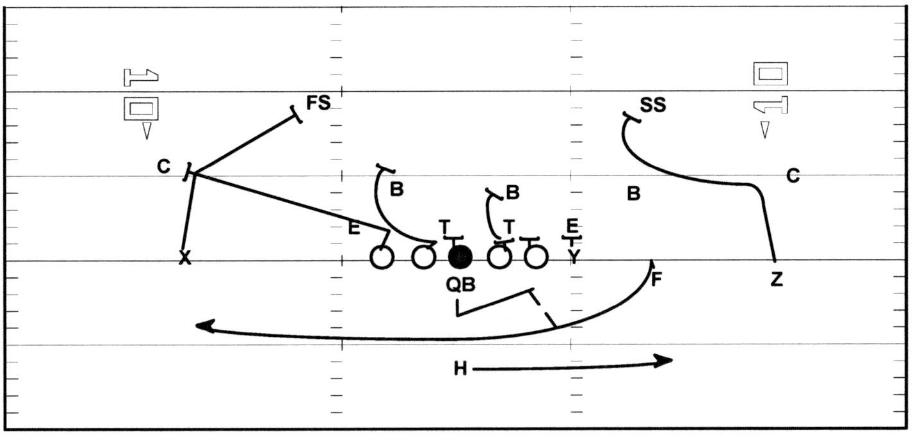

Description: The misdirection in this play results from the reverse off of the speed option action.

Assignments:

QB: Drop steps. Executes speed option right. Pitches to F.

H: Executes speed option track (great fake flash hands).

F: Runs reverse track. Secures the pitch.

Y: Zone blocks.

Z: Convoy blocks to the near safety.

X: Pushes and cracks the near safety.

LT: Steps to inside gap. Releases to block the flat defender.

LG: Slams defensive lineman. Releases to block second level flow.

C: Zone blocks.

RG: Combo blocks to second level.

RT: Combo blocks to second level.

Coaching Points: The QB and H must sell the speed option. The pitch must be executed at the proper mesh point.

Play #36: Sweep Right Reverse Left

Jeff Horton
University of Wisconsin

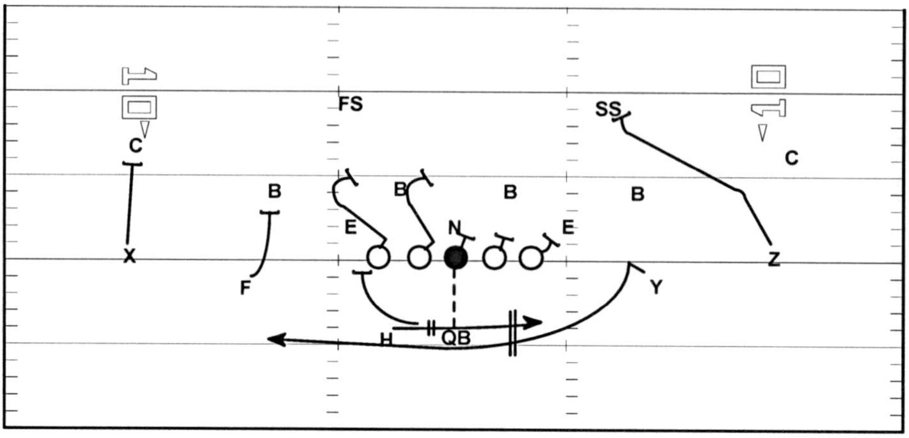

Description: This play offers great misdirection from the gun alignment.

Assignments:

QB: Aligns in gun. Hands off underneath to H. Protects backside flow.

H: Executes sweep right track. Secures handoff.

F: Blocks most dangerous second level defender.

Y: Executes reverse track. Secures handoff from H.

Z: Convoys to near safety.

X: Blocks man on.

LT: Steps to inside gap. Releases to block the alley.

LG: Slams defensive lineman. Releases to block second level flow.

C: Zone blocks.

RG: Zone blocks.

RT: Zone blocks.

Coaching Points: Y must have an 8- to 10-yard split to allow H to sell the run.

Play #37: Bounce Left Reverse Right

Dabo Swinney
Clemson University

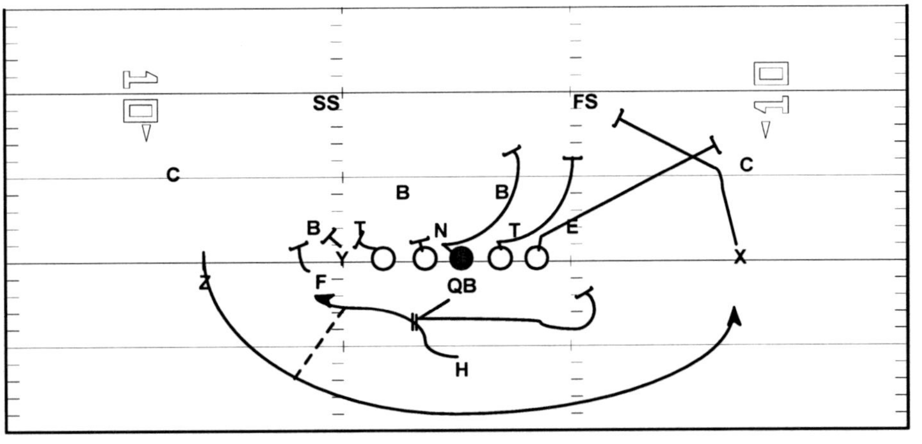

Description: This play offers great misdirection off of the bounce action.

Assignments:

QB: Opens. Executes handoff on bounce. Carries out naked and blocks backside flow.

H: Executes bounce track. Secures handoff. Pitches to Z on the reverse.

F: Blocks edge pressure.

Y: Executes zone blocking.

Z: Executes reverse track. Secures pitch. Gets depth.

X: Pushes and cracks the near safety.

LT: Executes zone blocking.

LG: Executes zone blocking.

C: Slams. Releases and blocks second level flow.

RG: Slams. Releases and blocks the alley.

RT: Jab steps to inside gap. Releases and blocks the flat defender.

Coaching Points: Z must have a 12-yard split to allow the H to sell the run to create defensive pursuit.

Play #38: Fake Zone Right Reverse Left

Charlie Stubbs
University of Central Missouri

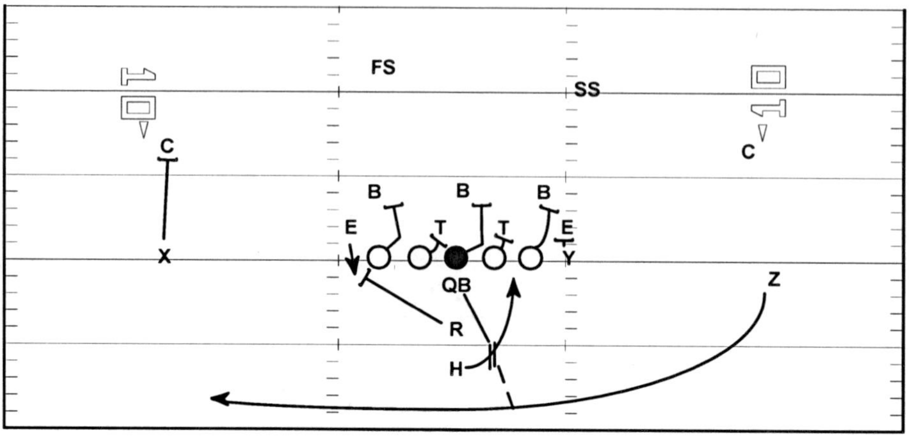

Description: This play is a misdirection off of the inside zone run getting the ball into a playmaker's hands.

Assignments:

QB: Open fakes inside zone right. Pitches the ball to Z on reverse.

H: Executes inside zone right track (great fake).

R: Blocks backside defensive end (possible cut outside thigh).

Y: Blocks inside zone right.

Z: Executes reverse track. Gets depth. Secures pitch.

X: Blocks most dangerous defender.

LT: Blocks inside zone right.

LG: Blocks inside zone right.

C: Blocks inside zone right.

RG: Blocks inside zone right.

RT: Blocks inside zone right.

Coaching Points: The reverse receiver (Z) must get depth to avoid backside defensive flow. This blocking scheme is the simplest. Z must be able to make at least one secondary support defender miss in the open field.

Play #39: Toss Right Reverse Left

Charlie Stubbs
University of Central Missouri

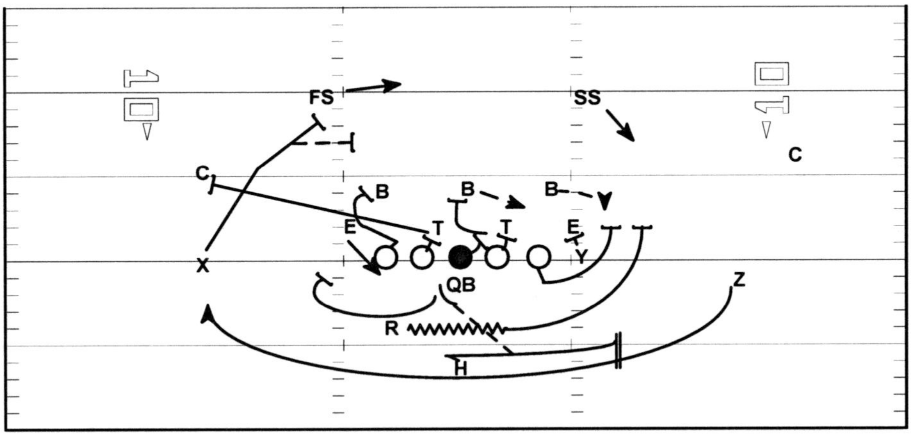

Description: This play is a reverse play off of the toss action versus a fast flowing defense.

Assignments:

QB: Reverses out. Executes toss right. Carries out naked. Assists blocking backside flow.

H: Executes toss right track. Secures ball and sells run. Hands the ball off to the reverse receiver (Z).

R: Motions short. Blocks support defender.

Y: Base blocks man on.

Z: Executes reverse track. Secures handoff.

X: Pushes and cracks the near safety.

LT: Releases inside. Blocks inside linebacker.

LG: Slams defensive lineman. Releases and blocks the flat defender.

C: Combo blocks.

RG: Combo blocks.

RT: Pulls to block flowing linebacker. Stays alert for a run through.

Coaching Points: The reverse receiver (Z) must get depth to avoid backside defensive flow.

Play #40: Fake Iso Reverse Left

Charlie Stubbs
University of Central Missouri

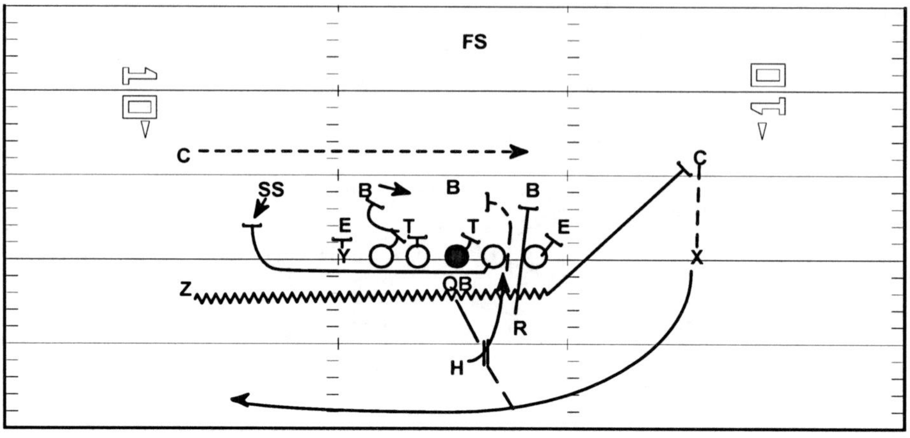

Description: This play provides a misdirection run versus an aggressive flowing defense. To be effective, the QB must execute a great iso fake (holding the defense) and then flip the ball to X (playmaker). This play is great against man coverage.

Assignments:

QB: Reverses out. Fakes iso. Pitches the ball to X on reverse.

H: Executes iso track (great fake). Possible chip blocks inside linebacker.

R: Executes iso block.

Y: Base blocks defensive end.

Z: Motions across. Blocks the most dangerous defender aligned on the X receiver.

X: Executes reverse track. Secures pitch.

LT: Combo blocks to second level flow.

LG: Combo blocks to second level flow.

C: Base blocks man on.

RG: Pulls left to block the secondary support.

RT: Base blocks man on.

Coaching Points: The reverse receiver (X) must get depth to avoid backside defensive flow.

Play #41: Fake Zone Left Reverse Right Pass

Charlie Stubbs
University of Alabama

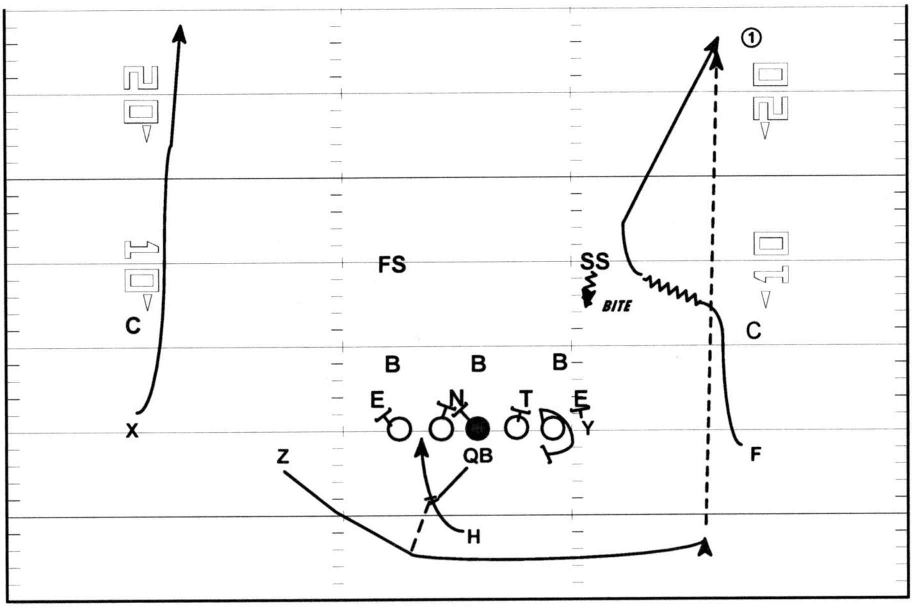

Description: This play is a misdirection reverse pass which provides an opportunity to utilize all of your playmaker's skills.

Assignments:

QB: Open fakes inside zone left. Flips ball to Z on reverse.

H: Runs inside zone left (great fake). Be alert for edge pressure (possible protection).

F: Fakes push crack blocks. Remains patient. Releases into route.

Y: Blocks man on.

Z: Executes reverse (gets depth). Reads F on route (run/pass option).

X: Releases on go route.

LT: Executes PAP protection (big on big).

LG: Executes PAP protection (big on big).

C: Executes PAP protection (blocks left).

RG: Executes PAP protection (big on big).

RT: Executes PAP protection (big on big). Uncovers possible seal block.

Coaching Points: Z must get depth from QB on flip (no set–up) and must throw on the run.

Play #42: Speed Sweep Left Reverse Right Pass

Charlie Stubbs
University of Tulsa

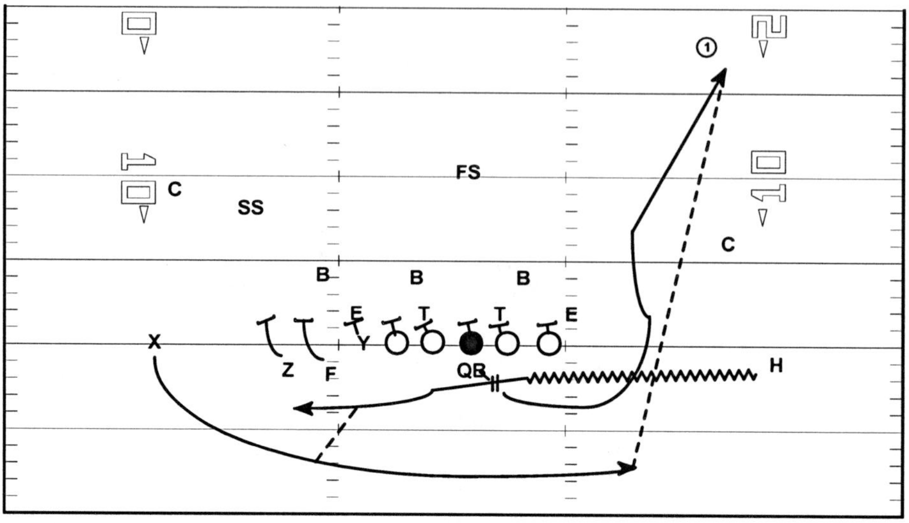

Description: This special play-action pass complements the speed sweep package. At times defenses will disregard the QB as a potential down the field receiver. This play offers a great opportunity to exploit that weakness.

Assignments:

QB: Open hands off speed sweep to H. Drifts weakside. Executes a corner route.

H: Motions. Receives handoff on speed sweep. Pitches to X.

F: Executes reach protection.

Y: Executes reach protection.

Z: Executes reach protection.

X: Executes reverse track. Receives pitch. Gains depth.

LT: Executes reach protection.

LG: Executes reach protection.

C: Executes reach protection.

RG: Executes reach protection.

RT: Executes reach protection.

Coaching Points: The split for X should be 10 to 12 yards. X must throw on the run. The primary target is the QB on the corner route. In this play X has a run/pass option.

Play #43: Reverse Pass Off Bounce Play

Dabo Swinney
Clemson University

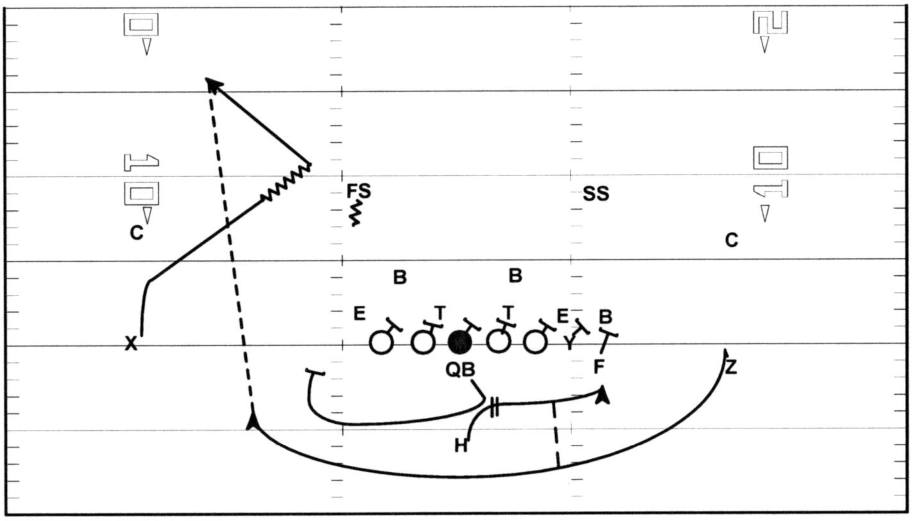

Description: The misdirection in this play will exploit an aggressive defensive flow and secondary. This play provides a great opportunity to utilize all of your playmakers' skills.

Assignments:

QB: Open hands off bounce (zone) play. Secures backside flow protection.

H: Executes bounce track. Secures handoff. Tosses the ball to Z on reverse.

F: Executes PAP reach protection. Seals the edge.

Y: Executes PAP reach protection.

Z: Executes reverse track. Gets depth. Receives toss. Pass/run option.

X: Fakes push/crack blocks of near safety. Executes corner route.

LT: Executes PAP reach protection.

LG: Executes PAP reach protection.

C: Executes PAP reach protection.

RG: Executes PAP reach protection.

RT: Executes PAP reach protection.

Coaching Points: Players must perfect and execute the ball handling required for this play. Z must be a great decision maker with a run or pass option.

Play #44: Lead Option Left Reverse Right Pass

Bob Toledo
UCLA

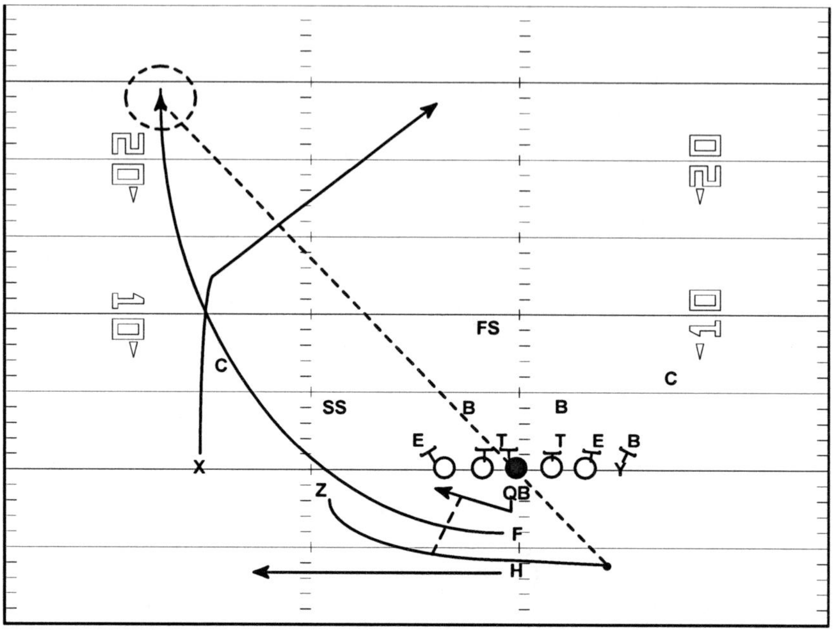

Description: This play complements offenses using basic option football. It provides an opportunity to attack flowing defenses using a playmaker's abilities.

Assignments:

QB: Drops back. Opens. Executes lead option. Pitches to reverse receiver (Z).

H: Executes lead option track. Gets width.

F: Releases as lead blocker. Executes a wide arc route.

Y: Executes PAP protection (solid).

Z: Executes reverse (sells run). Sets up for throwback to F.

X: Executes a pole route (opposite hash).

LT: Executes PAP protection (solid).

LG: Executes PAP protection (solid).

C: Executes PAP protection (solid).

RG: Executes PAP protection (solid).

RT: Executes PAP protection (solid).

Coaching Points: Z must be an excellent passer. After taking the pitch, the flanker pulls up nine yards deep over OT. The throw will be a 30+ yard pass to F.

Play #45: Zone Right Fake Reverse Pass—Ex. 1

Charlie Stubbs
University of Alabama

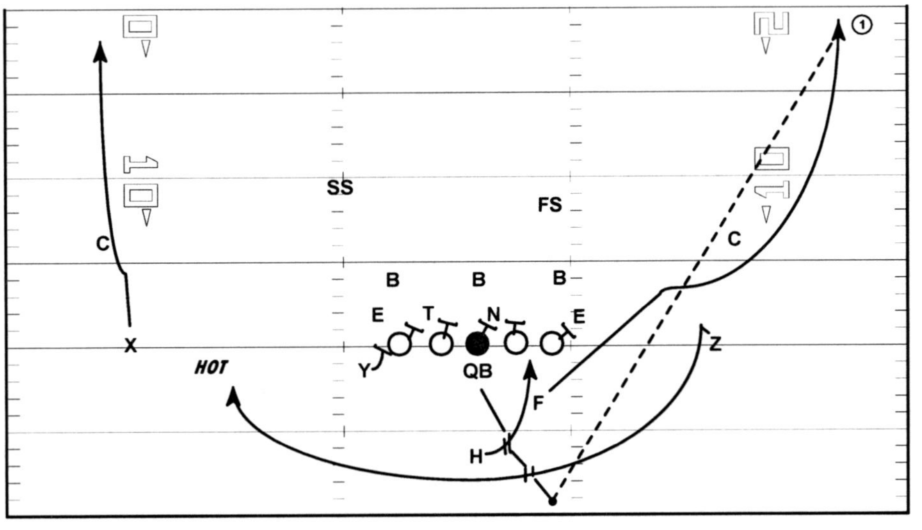

Description: This play complements the reverse package with additional backfield actions. It is best used on first downs against more passive or zone defenses.

Assignments:

QB: Open fakes inside zone right. Fakes reverse to Z. Gains ground. Sets up in C gap (9 to 10 yards deep).

H: Executes zone track. Provides protection key the inside linebacker.

F: Executes wheel route.

Y: Checks protection. Helps.

Z: Executes reverse track (great fake).

X: Releases outside on go route.

LT: Executes PAP protection (aggressive).

LG: Executes PAP protection (aggressive).

C: Executes PAP protection (aggressive).

RG: Executes PAP protection (aggressive).

RT: Executes PAP protection (aggressive).

Coaching Points: The QB must execute great fakes. The primary target is F on the wheel route. Z is the hot receiver.

Play #46: Zone Right Fake Reverse Pass—Ex. 2

Charlie Stubbs
University of Alabama

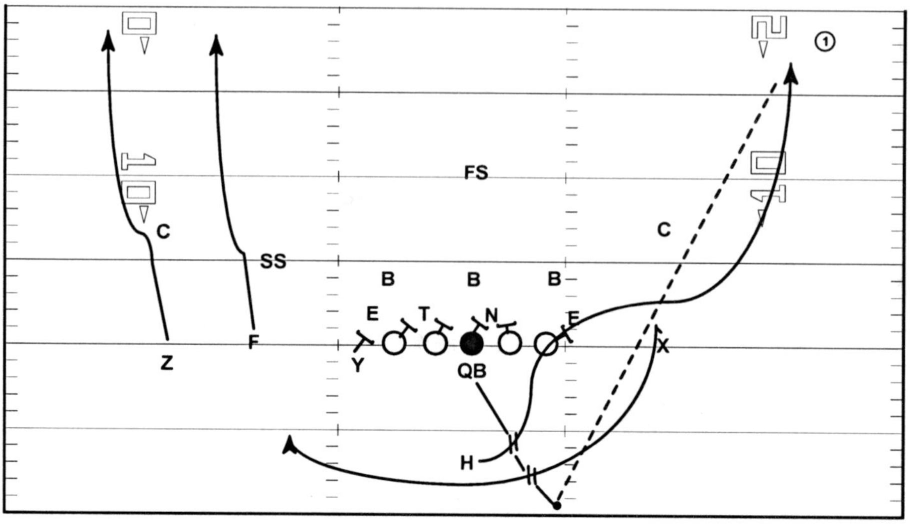

Description: This play is a down the field play-action pass offering great misdirection. A great play into the boundary and on first down.

Assignments:

QB: Open fakes inside zone right. Fakes reverse. Gains ground and drifts.

H: Fakes inside zone right. Executes wheel route.

F: Releases outside on go route.

Y: Executes gap protection (rip).

Z: Releases outside on go route.

X: Runs reverse track (great fake).

LT: Executes gap protection (rip).

LG: Executes gap protection (rip).

C: Executes gap protection (rip).

RG: Executes gap protection (rip).

RT: Executes gap protection (rip).

Coaching Points: The QB must execute great fakes. The primary target is H on the wheel route.

Play #47: Fake Zone and Reverse Wheel Route

Charlie Stubbs
University of Alabama

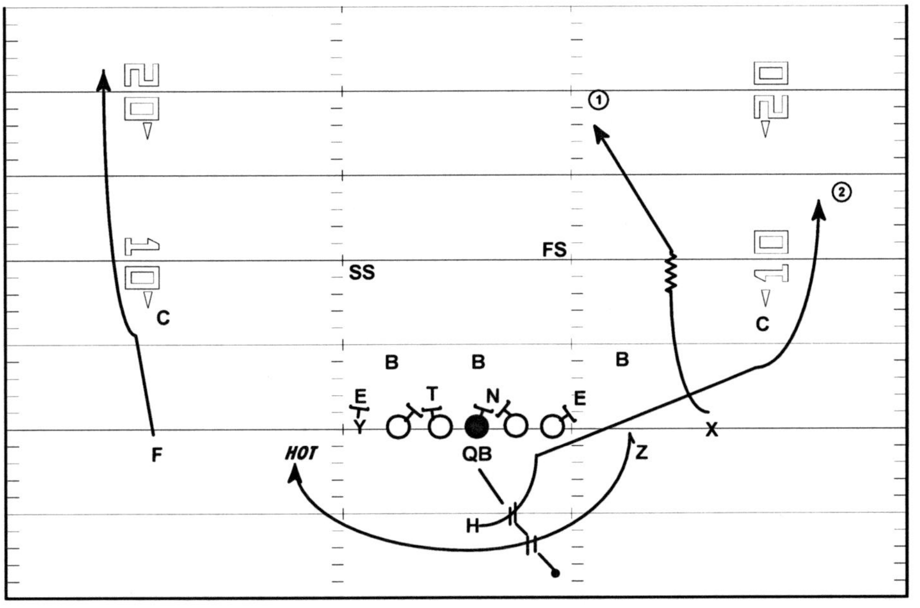

Description: This play is a down the field play-action pass with the wheel concept offering great misdirection. This play is a good play for in the middle of the field and on first down.

Assignments:

QB: Open fakes inside zone right. Fakes reverse. Gains ground and drifts.

H: Fakes inside zone. Executes arrow and up route. Gets width.

F: Releases outside on go route.

Y: Executes PAP protection (aggressive).

Z: Executes reverse track (great fake). Possible hot.

X: Executes a stutter post route.

LT: Executes PAP protection (aggressive).

LG: Executes PAP protection (aggressive).

C: Executes PAP protection (aggressive).

RG: Executes PAP protection (aggressive).

RT: Executes PAP protection (aggressive).

Coaching Points: The QB must execute great fakes. The progression is X (post) to H (arrow & up). Z is the hot receiver.

Play #48: Fake Zone and Reverse Pass

Charlie Stubbs
University of Tulsa

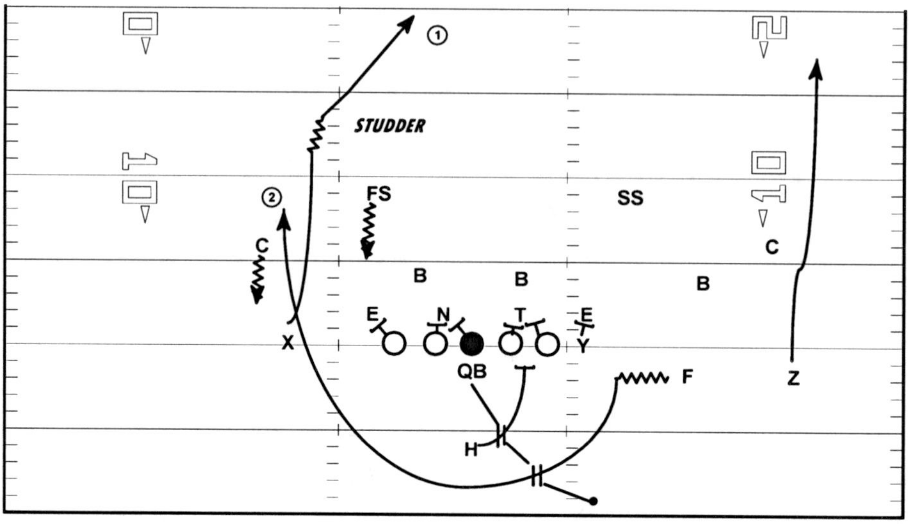

Description: This deep play-action pass is very effective versus aggressive safety play or rotation in the secondary.

Assignments:

QB: Open fakes inside zone right. Fakes reverse. Gains ground. Sets up 9 to 10 yards deep in the C gap.

H: Executes inside zone track (great fake). Possibly helps protect.

F: Executes motion. Fakes reverse. Executes wide swing route.

Y: Executes inside zone PAP protection (firm).

Z: Releases outside on go route.

X: Executes a stutter post route.

LT: Executes inside zone PAP protection (firm).

LG: Executes inside zone PAP protection (firm).

C: Executes inside zone PAP protection (firm).

RG: Executes inside zone PAP protection (firm).

RT: Executes inside zone PAP protection (firm).

Coaching Points: The QB progression is X (post) to F (swing).

Play #49: Zone Right Fake Reverse H Wheel

Charlie Stubbs
University of Tulsa

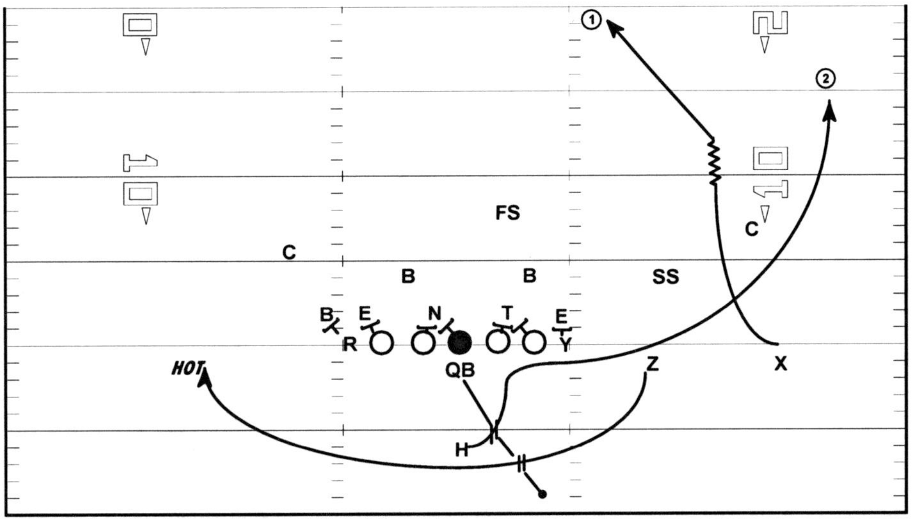

Description: This misdirection play-action pass has the ability to get the ball deep down the field.

Assignments:

QB: Open fakes inside zone right. Fakes reverse. Drifts and gains ground to the C gap (sets up 9 to 10 yards deep.)

H: Fakes inside zone right. Releases on wheel route.

R: Executes PAP protection (solid).

Y: Executes PAP protection (solid).

Z: Fakes reverse. Possible hot receiver.

X: Executes a stutter post route.

LT: Executes PAP protection (solid).

LG: Executes PAP protection (solid).

C: Executes PAP protection (solid).

RG: Executes PAP protection (solid).

RT: Executes PAP protection (solid).

Coaching Points: QB progression is X (post) to H (wheel). Z is a possible hot receiver. Everyone must execute great fakes.

Play #50: Fake Lead Left Reverse Throwback

Mike Empey
Brigham Young University

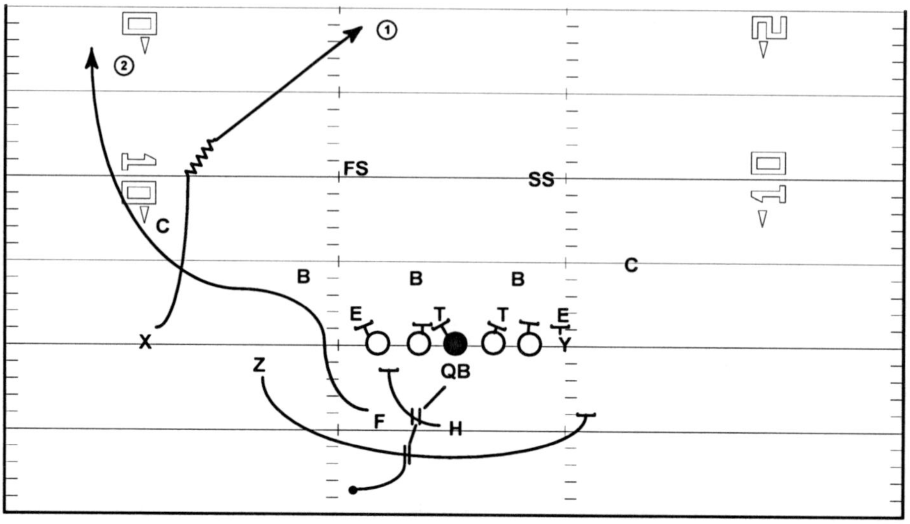

Description: This special pass is a double play fake off of a weakside lead, then reverse. The fullback is able to release undetected or in the open field versus a linebacker.

Assignments:

QB: Open fakes leads left. Fakes reverse. Sets up seven to nine yards deep in the C gap.

H: Fakes leads left. Checks protection. Helps.

F: Free releases. Executes wheel route.

Y: Executes solid protection.

Z: Fakes reverse. Possible backside protection.

X: Executes a stutter post route.

LT: Executes solid protection.

LG: Executes solid protection.

C: Executes solid protection.

RG: Executes solid protection.

RT: Executes solid protection.

Coaching Points: The QB progression is X (stutter post) to F (wheel route).

5

Special Play-Action Passes

Harry How/Getty Images

Play #51: Toss Right Halfback Pass—Ex. 1

Charlie Stubbs
University of Alabama

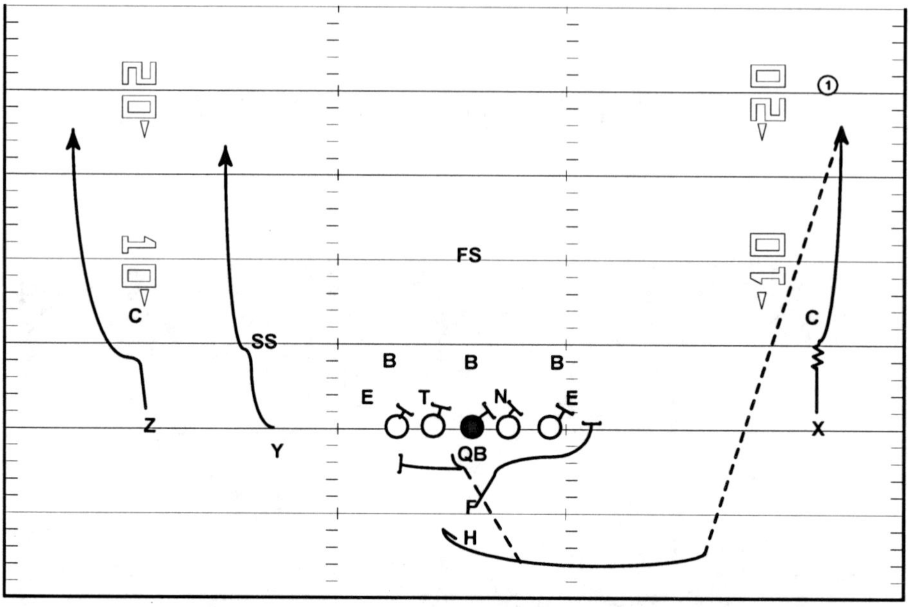

Description: This play provides an opportunity to utilize all of your playmakers' skills. Reminder: The back (H) must be a very good decision maker.

Assignments:

QB: Reverses out. Executes toss. Blocks backside edge pressure.

H: Jab steps. Executes toss track (runs four to five strides parallel to LOS). Pass/run option.

F: Blocks support defender. Cannot block downfield.

Y: Releases outside on go route.

Z: Releases outside on go route.

X: Executes stalk and go route (is patient).

LT: Executes PAP protection (toss action).

LG: Executes PAP protection (toss action).

C: Executes PAP protection (toss action).

RG: Executes PAP protection (toss action).

RT: Executes PAP protection (toss action).

Coaching Points: The halfback progression is X as a primary target, but it is a pass/run option play.

Play #52: Toss Right Halfback Pass—Ex. 2

Charlie Stubbs
University of Central Missouri

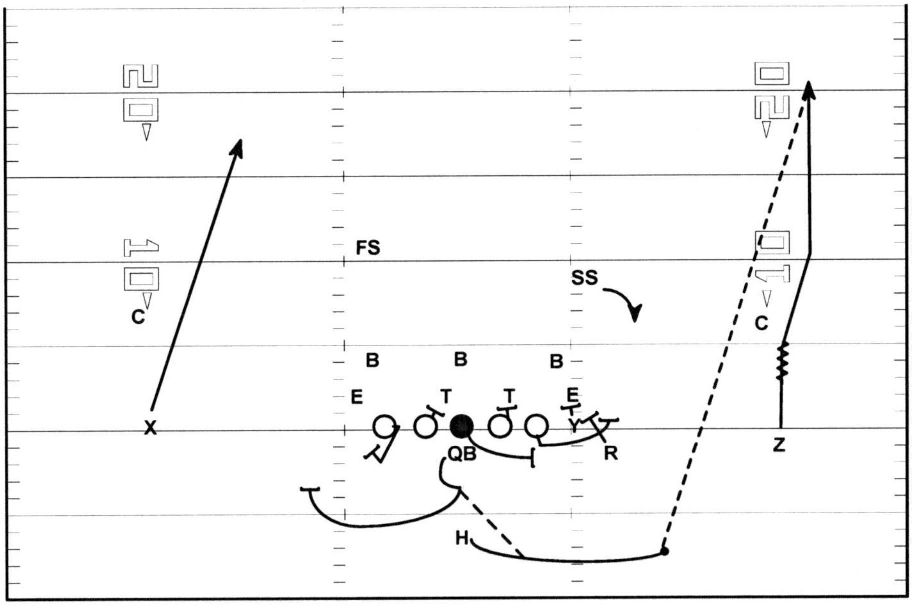

Description: This play is great versus quick and aggressive secondary support.

Assignments:

QB: Reverses out. Executes toss. Protects backside flow.

H: Secures toss (sells run four or five strides).

R: Executes PAP protection (toss).

Y: Executes PAP protection (toss).

Z: Executes a stalk and go route (is patient).

X: Runs a seam route (influences the free safety).

LT: Executes PAP protection (toss).

LG: Executes PAP protection (toss).

C: Executes PAP protection (toss).

RG: Executes PAP protection (toss).

RT: Executes PAP protection (toss).

Coaching Points: H has a pass or run option; therefore, he must make a great decision.

Play #53: Fake Draw Running Back Seam

Charlie Stubbs
University of Alabama

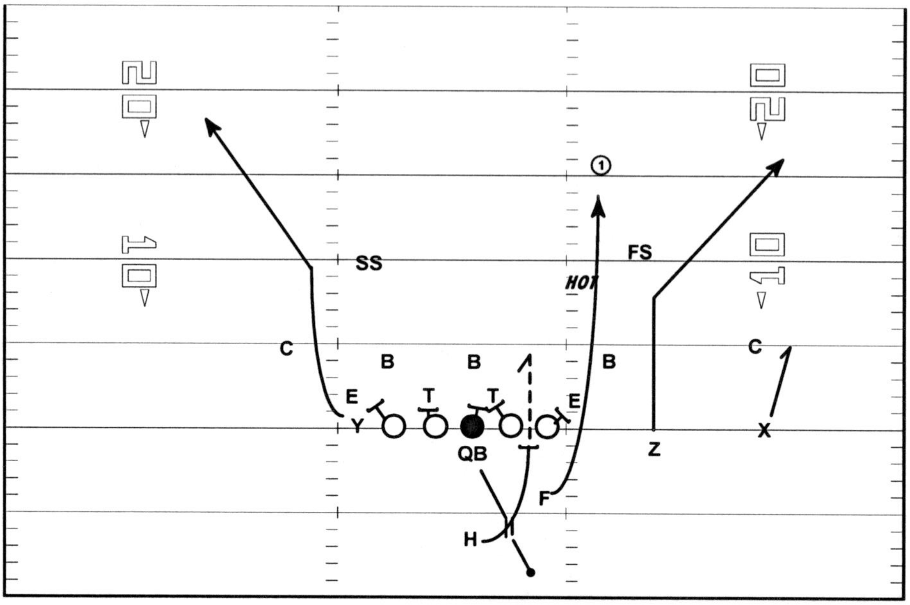

Description: This play is a special PAP versus two high safeties (cover 2 or 4) or a blitz. This play is an excellent choice in the red zone.

Assignments:

QB: Open fakes draw. Sets up.

H: Fakes draw. Checks protection. Releases on hook route (three yards).

F: Aligns wider behind OT. Takes best release on middle seam route. Possible hot receiver.

Y: Executes a corner route.

Z: Executes a corner route.

X: Runs a smash route (five yard depth).

LT: Executes dropback protection (five step).

LG: Executes dropback protection (five step).

C: Executes dropback protection (five step).

RG: Executes dropback protection (five step).

RT: Executes dropback protection (five step).

Coaching Points: The QB progression varies based on coverage. For two high safeties, the progression reads F to Z to X. For one high safety, the progression reads X to Z. Versus blitz, the possible hots are F or X. The QB needs to execute a great draw fake to influence the linebackers.

Play #54: Fake Iso Right Wheel Route

Charlie Stubbs
University of Tulsa

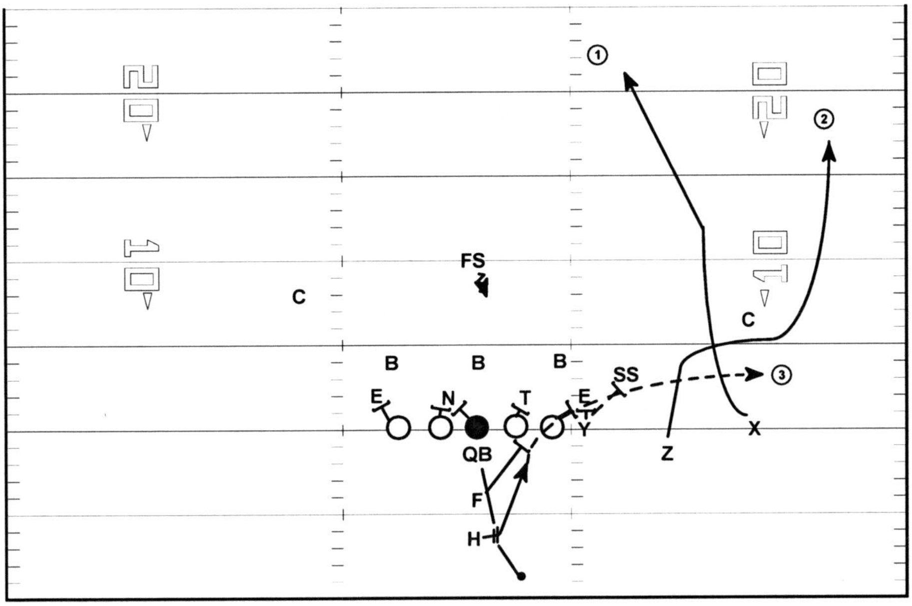

Description: This deep down the field play-action pass is excellent versus aggressive safeties. It is a great selection in short yardage situations.

Assignments:

QB: Reverses out. Fakes iso right (sets up 9 to 10 yards deep in the B gap).

H: Executes iso track (great fake). Then releases on a flat route.

F: Executes iso track. Protection (first inside LB playside).

Y: Executes PAP protection (iso) .

Z: Executes wheel route.

X: Executes post route.

LT: Executes PAP protection (iso) .

LG: Executes PAP protection (iso).

C: Executes PAP protection (iso).

RG: Executes PAP protection (iso).

RT: Executes PAP protection (iso).

Coaching Points: The QB progression is X (post) to Z (wheel). H has a check down route in the flat area.

Play #55: Fake Speed Sweep and Zone Y Sneak

Charlie Stubbs
University of Tulsa

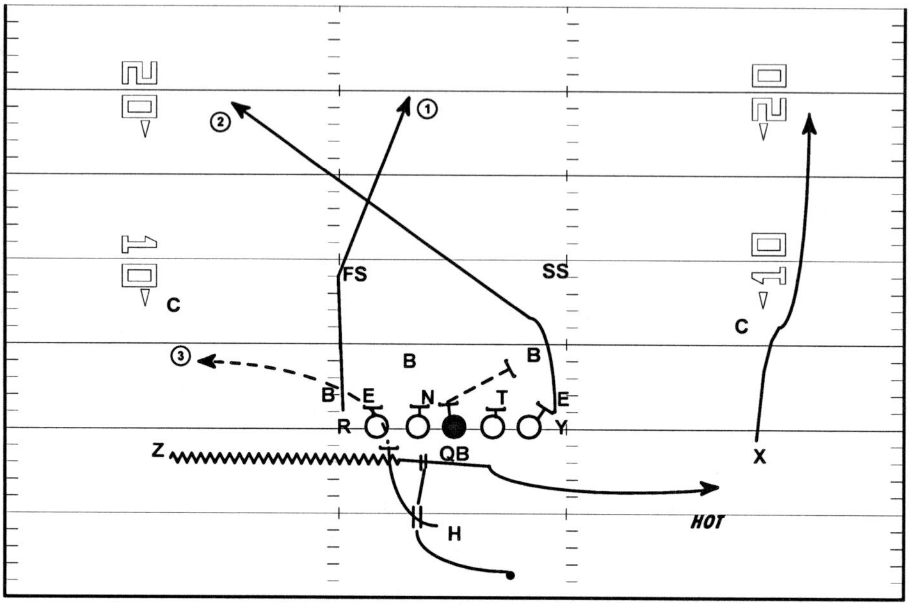

Description: This play-action pass provides excellent misdirection and utilizes TEs that have great speed.

Assignments:

QB: Open fakes speed sweep. Fakes inside zone left. Executes naked right (sets up seven to nine yards in the C gap).

H: Executes inside zone left (great fake). Checks protection (inside linebacker to outside). Releases on flat route.

R: Executes best release. Runs a skinny post route.

Y: Executes an over route (climbing to a depth of 22 yards).

Z: Motions. Fakes speed sweep. Bubbles (possible hot receiver).

X: Executes a go route.

LT: Executes inside zone PAP protection.

LG: Executes inside zone PAP protection.

C: Executes inside zone PAP protection.

RG: Executes inside zone PAP protection.

RT: Executes inside zone PAP protection.

Coaching Points: The QB progression is R (skinny post) to Y (over route) to H (flat). Z is a possible hot receiver. To be successful, there must be great fakes.

Play #56: Option Right Pass

Fisher DeBerry
Air Force Academy

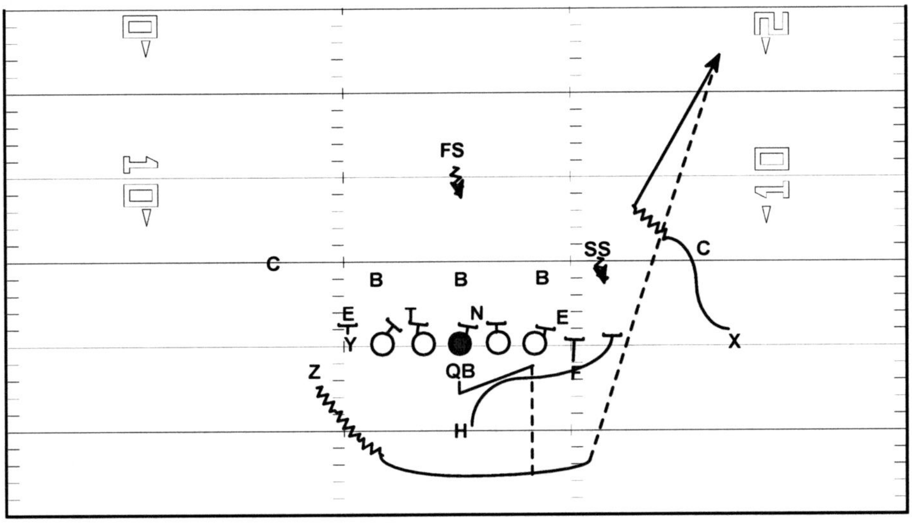

Description: This play is a great complement for option offenses to exploit quick secondary support as opponents work to defend the option attack.

Assignments:

QB: Executes option phase. Pitches.

H: Leads option. Blocks support defender at LOS.

F: Blocks and seals the edge.

Y: Executes reach protection.

Z: Motions to option and pitch phase. Executes pass or run option.

X: Fakes push and crack to near safety. Executes corner route.

LT: Executes reach protection.

LG: Executes reach protection.

C: Executes reach protection.

RG: Executes reach protection.

RT: Executes reach protection.

Coaching Points: Z (option back) must make the decision (pass or run) on the move. He must not set up.

Play #57: Unbalanced Right Zone Right Pass

Mike Empey
Brigham Young University

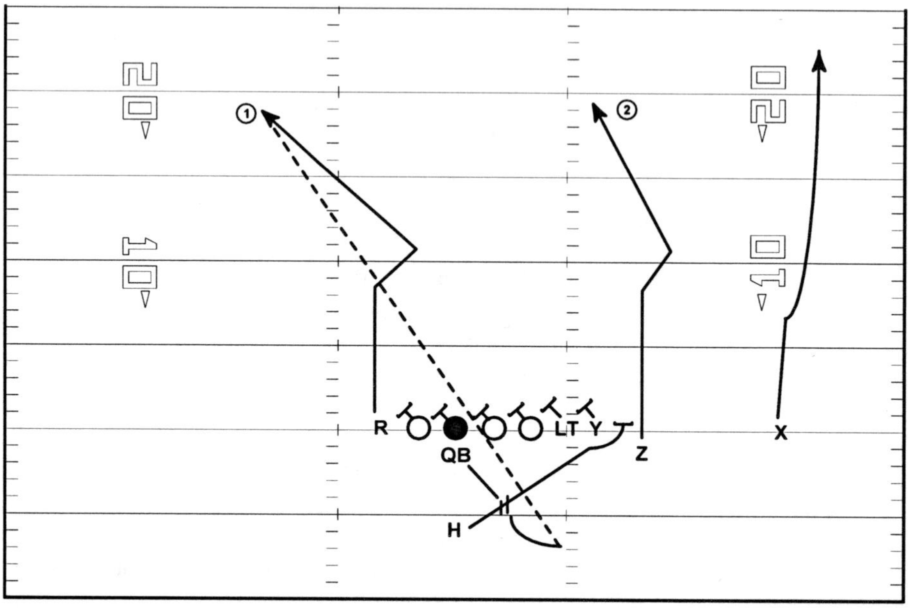

Description: This pass play is an unbalanced run fake play-action pass. The object is to get the weak TE out on a pass route undetected. The play is called in the huddle, and the team sprints to the LOS, snaps the ball quickly so the defense doesn't notice the alignment changes of the weak tackle and TE.

Assignments:

QB: Open fakes bounce. Sets up seven to nine yards deep in the C gap.

H: Fakes bounce right. Blocks edge pressure.

R: Executes best release. Runs a corner route. Aligns next to left guard (hides jersey number).

Y: Executes gap protection (Liz).

Z: Executes a corner post route.

X: Releases outside on a go route.

LT: Aligns unbalanced tackle over. Executes gap protection (Liz).

LG: Executes gap protection (Liz).

C: Executes gap protection (Liz).

RG: Executes gap protection (Liz).

RT: Executes gap protection (Liz).

Coaching Points: The QB progression is R (corner) to Z (post).

Play #58: Fake Zone Left Z Dagger—Ex. 1

Charlie Stubbs
University of Louisville

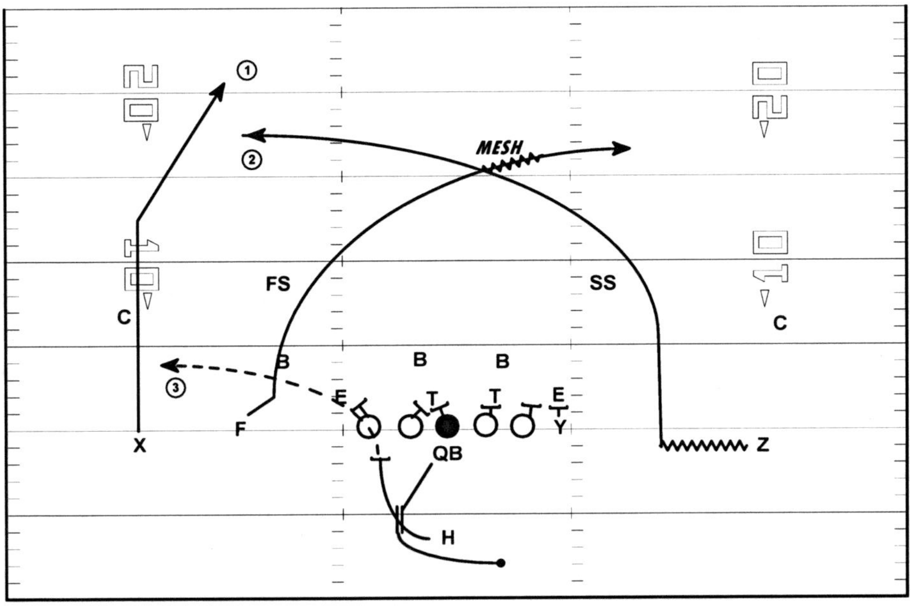

Description: This deep play-action pass is off of the inside zone fake. The play is great versus zone coverage with aggressive safeties. It is also excellent versus man coverage with a potential rub (down the field).

Assignments:

QB: Open fakes inside zone. Sets up 5 to 7 yards behind OT.

H: Executes inside zone track (great fake). Checks protection then releases on a flat route.

F: Stems up the field on mesh route (depth 12 to 15 yards). Possibly rubs for Z.

Y: Executes solid protection.

Z: Motions inside. Stems to dagger route. Responsible for the rub underneath F. Climbs after mesh to depth of 22 yards.

X: Executes a post route.

LT: Executes PAP protection (inside zone).

LG: Executes PAP protection (inside zone).

C: Executes PAP protection (inside zone).

RG: Executes solid protection.

RT: Executes solid protection.

Coaching Points: The QB progression is X (post) to Z (dagger) to H (flat).

Play #59: Fake Zone Left Z Dagger—Ex. 2

Charlie Stubbs
University of Louisville

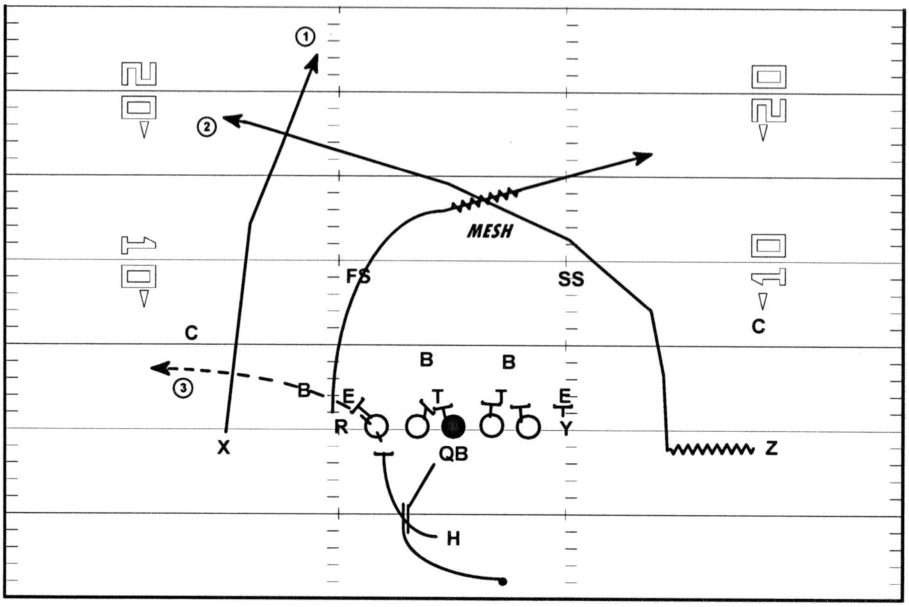

Description: This deep play-action pass is off of the inside zone fake. The play is great versus zone coverage with aggressive safeties. It is also excellent versus man coverage with a potential rub (down the field).

Assignments:

QB: Open fakes inside zone. Sets up five to seven yards behind OT.

H: Executes inside zone track (great fake). Checks protection then releases on a flat route.

R: Executes best release on mesh route (depth 12 to 15 yards). Possibly rubs for Z.

Y: Executes solid protection.

Z: Motions inside. Stems to dagger route. Responsible for the rub underneath R. Climbs after mesh to depth of 22 yards.

X: Executes a post route.

LT: Executes PAP protection (inside zone).

LG: Executes PAP protection (inside zone).

C: Executes PAP protection (inside zone).

RG: Executes solid protection.

RT: Executes solid protection.

Coaching Points: The QB progression X (post) to Z (dagger) to H (flat).

Play #60: Unbalanced Fake Iso Right Firm Dipper

Charlie Stubbs
University of Central Missouri

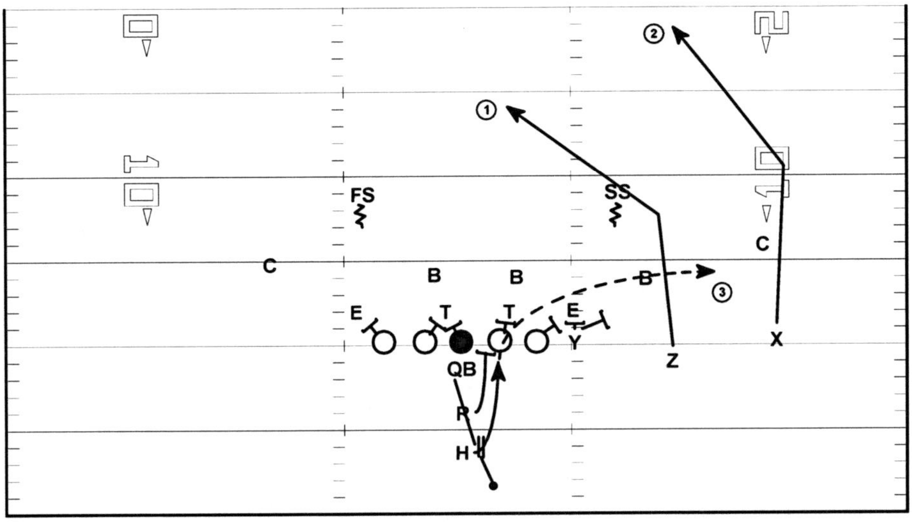

Description: The fake iso (lead) in this deep play-action pass is great versus aggressive defenses.

Assignments:

QB: Reverses out. Fakes iso (sets up 9 to 10 yards deep in the B gap).

H: Executes iso track (great fake). Possibly releases on a flat route.

R: Executes PAP protection (iso).

Y: Executes PAP protection (iso). Keys the edge pressure.

Z: Executes a post route (breaking point eight yards).

X: Executes a post route (breaking point 12 yards).

T: Executes PAP protection (iso).

LG: Executes PAP protection (iso).

C: Executes PAP protection (iso).

RG: Executes PAP protection (iso).

RT: Executes PAP protection (iso).

Coaching Points: The QB progression is Z (inside post) to X (outside post) to H.

Play #61: Fake Dive Right Double Pass

Charlie Stubbs
University of Central Missouri

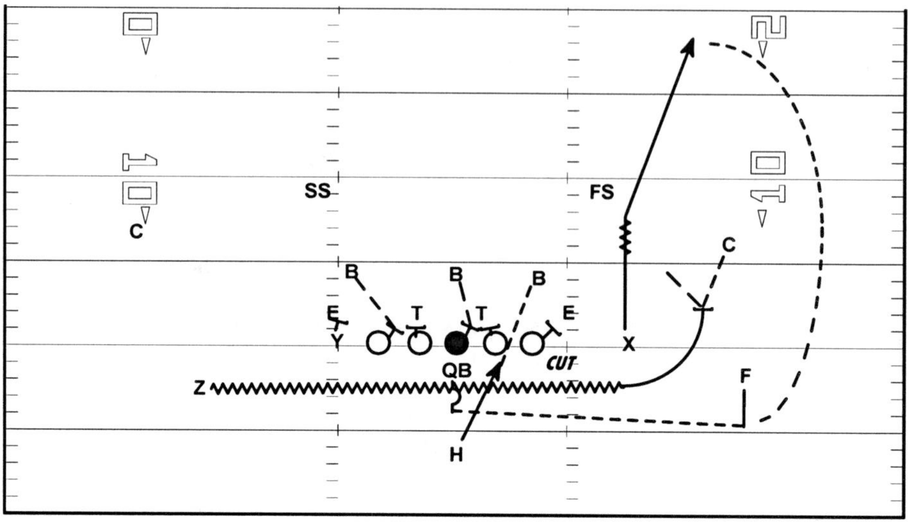

Description: With first a fake dive, then a double pass, this play offers a great opportunity to use your playmakers' athletic ability.

Assignments:

QB: Open flash fakes dive. Throws pass to F.

H: Executes dive track (great fake). Checks protection.

F: Drops back two yards from initial alignment. Executes pass or run option.

Y: Executes PAP protection (zone).

Z: Motions. Blocks most dangerous defender aligned near F.

X: Executes a stalk corner route.

LT: Executes PAP protection (zone).

LG: Executes PAP protection (zone).

C: Executes PAP protection (zone).

RG: Executes PAP protection (zone).

RT: Cuts defensive end – outside thigh is the target.

Coaching Points: QB must throw the ball backwards to F (lateral). F must make a great decision –run or pass.

6

Special Move the Pocket Plays: Roll-Outs, Bootlegs, and Nakeds

Wesley Hitt/Getty Images

Play #62: Dash Right Bomb

Charlie Stubbs
University of Alabama

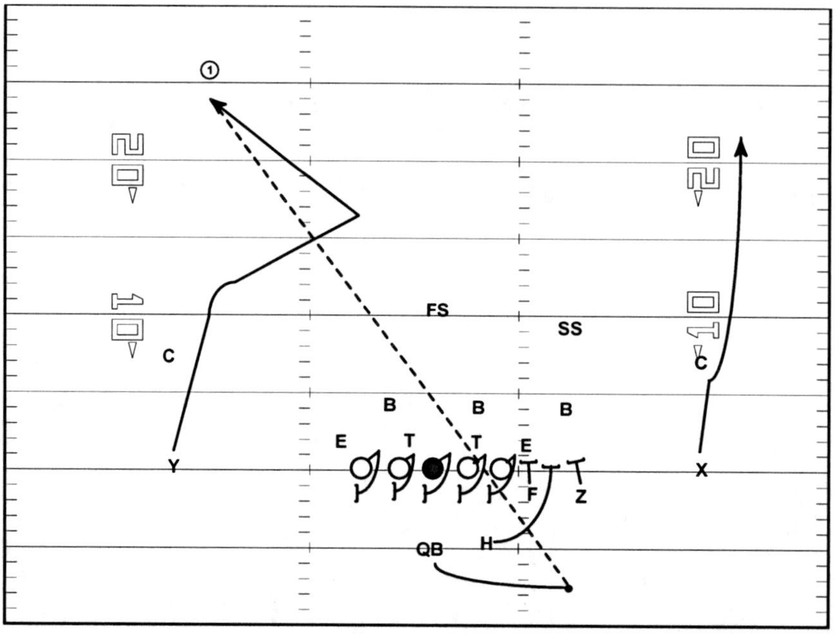

Description: Dash movement by the QB will give the time necessary for this deep throw. This play is excellent versus defenses that rotate, leaving the deep outside third of the field uncovered.

Assignments:

QB: Aligns in gun. After the snap, dashes right. Sets up.

H: Executes sprint protection. Blocks edge.

F: Executes sprint protection.

Y: Executes deep post corner route.

Z: Blocks man on.

X: Releases outside on go route.

LT: Executes sprint protection (hinge).

LG: Executes sprint protection (hinge).

C: Executes sprint protection (hinge).

RG: Executes sprint protection (hinge).

RT: Executes sprint protection (hinge).

Coaching Points: The QB must have a strong arm. The primary target is Y (deep post corner route).

Play #63: Reach Right Tight End Hide

Charlie Stubbs
University of Tulsa

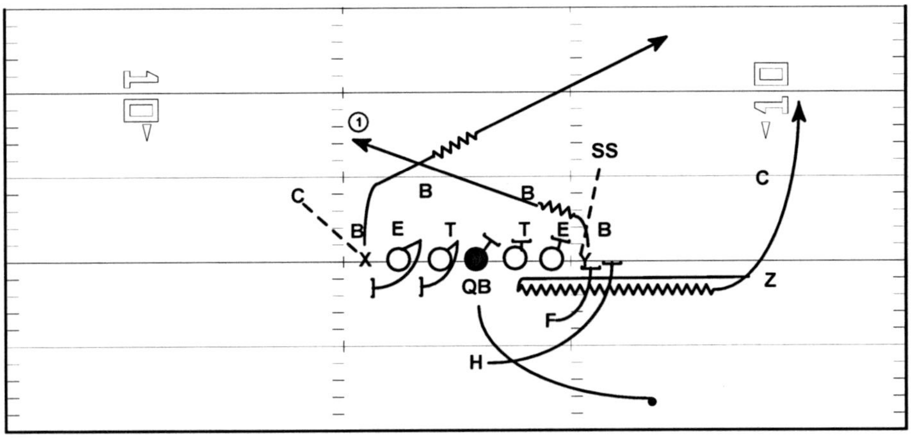

Description: This is a great play in short yardage and red zone situations. The tight end must be a great actor (deceptive).

Assignments:

QB: Executes sprintout right. Gains depth.

H: Executes sprint protection.

F: Executes sprint protection.

Y: Releases inside. Hides (falls down). Sneaks across to weakside area (looks for rub).

Z: Motions zorro (tip on coverage). Releases outside on fade route.

X: Executes best release. Sets depth of mesh route (possible rub for Y).

LT: Executes sprint protection (hinge).

LG: Executes sprint protection (hinge).

C: Executes sprint protection.

RG: Executes sprint protection.

RT: Executes sprint protection.

Coaching Points: QB must sprint out and gain ground to throw on the move. This play is an all or nothing play! QB must be reminded that if Y is not clearly open, then he should throw the ball away.

Play #64: Fake Sweep Right Bootleg Left Throwback—Pro Set

Dave Kragthorpe
Oregon State University

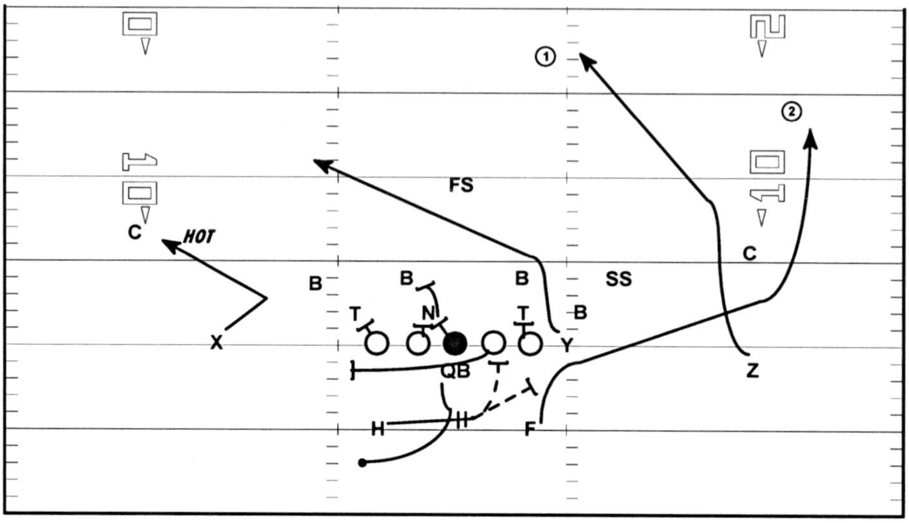

Description: This play is a deep play-action pass with the post and wheel concept. The boot protection will give the QB much needed time to read down the field.

Assignments:

QB: Reverses out. Fakes sweep (sets up five to seven yards deep weakside).

H: Executes sweep track (possible protection versus dog – double read).

F: Fakes cut block. Releases on an arrow and up route.

Y: Executes an over route (depth 8 to 10 yards).

Z: Executes a post route.

X: Executes a pivot route (hot receiver).

LT: Executes PAP boot left protection.

LG: Executes PAP boot left protection.

C: Executes PAP boot left protection.

RG: Executes PAP boot left protection.

RT: Executes PAP boot left protection.

Coaching Points: The QB progression is Z (post) to F (arrow and up). X is the hot receiver.

Play #65: Fake Sweep Right Bootleg Left Throwback—Boundary—Slot Formation

Dave Kragthorpe
Oregon State University

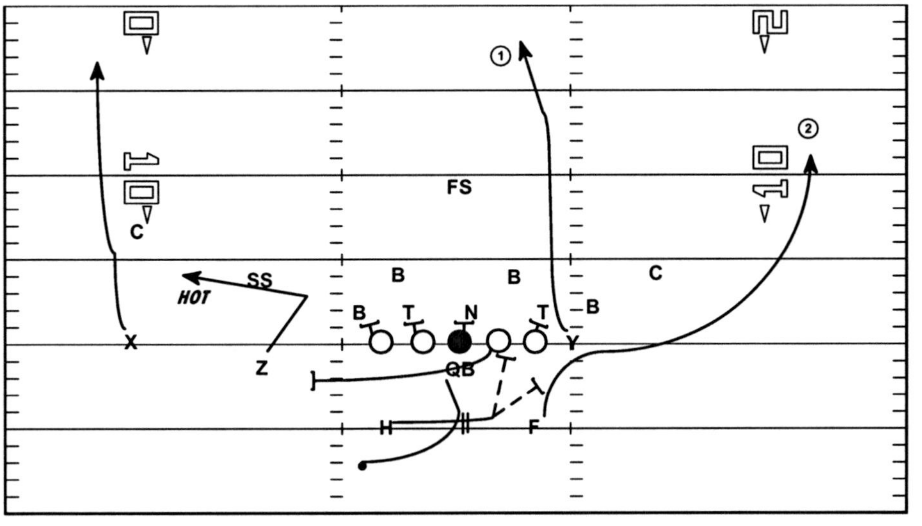

Description: This deep play-action pass has the post and wheel concept which is great into the boundary and red zone area. The boot protection will give the QB much needed time to read down the field.

Assignments:

QB: Reverses out. Fakes sweep (sets up five to seven yards deep weakside).

H: Executes sweep track (possible protection versus dog—double read).

F: Fakes cut block. Releases on an arrow and up route.

Y: Executes a skinny post route.

Z: Executes a pivot route (hot receiver).

X: Releases outside on a go route.

LT: Executes PAP boot left protection.

LG: Executes PAP boot left protection.

C: Executes PAP boot left protection.

RG: Executes PAP boot left protection.

RT: Executes PAP boot left protection.

Coaching Points: The QB progression is Y (skinny post) to F (arrow and up). Z is the hot receiver.

Play #66: Zone Left Naked Right Throwback—Ex. 1

Charlie Stubbs
University of Tulsa

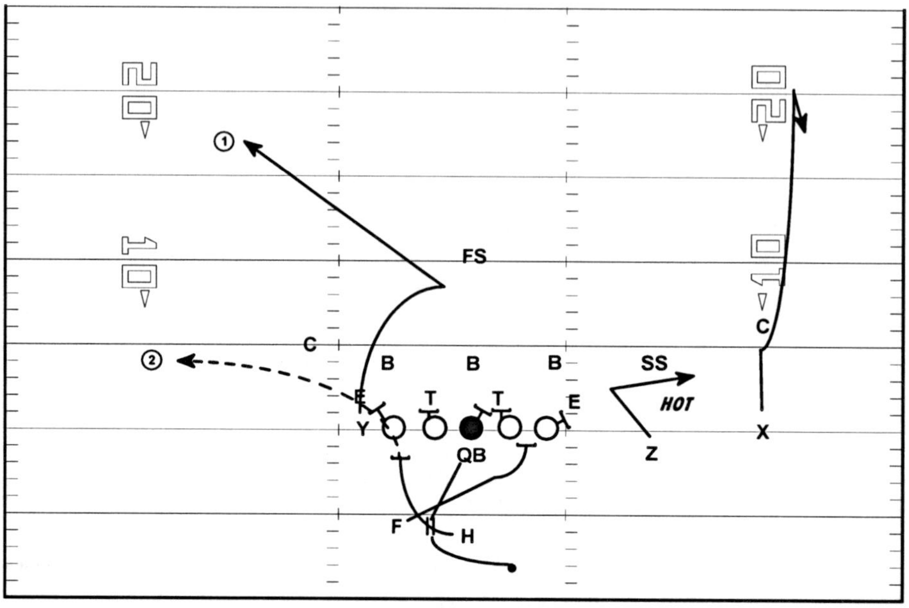

Description: This play-action pass complements the basic naked pass series. It is a great play in the red zone area utilizing this formation.

Assignments:

QB: Open fakes inside zone. Carries out naked right (sets up seven to nine yards in the B gap).

H: Executes zone left track (great fake). Checks protection. Releases on flat route.

F: Crosses underneath QB. Checks protection (inside LB to outside LB).

Y: Releases best. Executes throwback route (8 to angle at 22 yards).

Z: Executes pivot route (hot).

X: Executes a comeback route (18 to 15 yards).

LT: Executes throwback PAP protection.

LG: Executes throwback PAP protection.

C: Executes throwback PAP protection.

RG: Executes throwback PAP protection.

RT: Executes throwback PAP protection.

Coaching Points: The QB progression is Y (throwback route) to H (flat route). Z is hot.

Play #67: Zone Left Naked Right Throwback—Ex. 2

Charlie Stubbs
University of Tulsa/University of Central Missouri

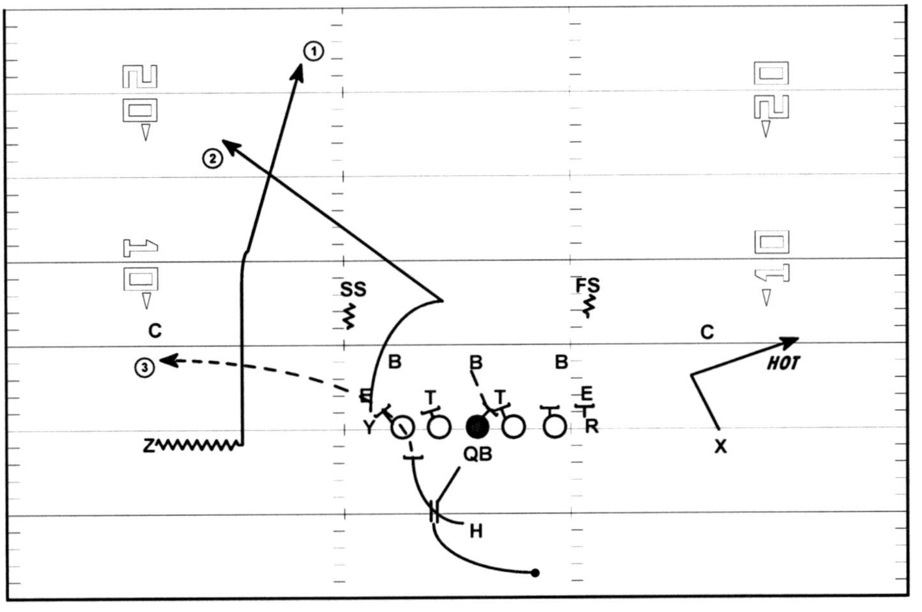

Description: This play is a deep play-action pass off of the inside zone play fake. This play is best utilized into the boundary with a three-layered vertical stretch.

Assignments:

QB: Open fakes inside zone left. Carries out naked (sets up seven to nine yards behind the OT).

H: Executes inside zone left track (great fake). Checks protection. Releases on a flat route.

R: Executes PAP protection (zone).

Y: Releases best. Executes a throwback route (8 yards to angle at 22 yards).

Z: Carries out short motion. Executes a skinny post route.

X: Executes a pivot route (hot).

LT: Executes PAP protection (inside zone).

LG: Executes PAP protection (inside zone).

C: Executes PAP protection (inside zone).

RG: Executes PAP protection (zone).

RT: Executes PAP protection (zone).

Coaching Points: The QB read progression is Z (post) to Y (throwback route) to H (flat). The hot receiver is X on the pivot route.

Play #68: Zone Left Naked Right Throwback—Ex. 3

Charlie Stubbs
University of Tulsa

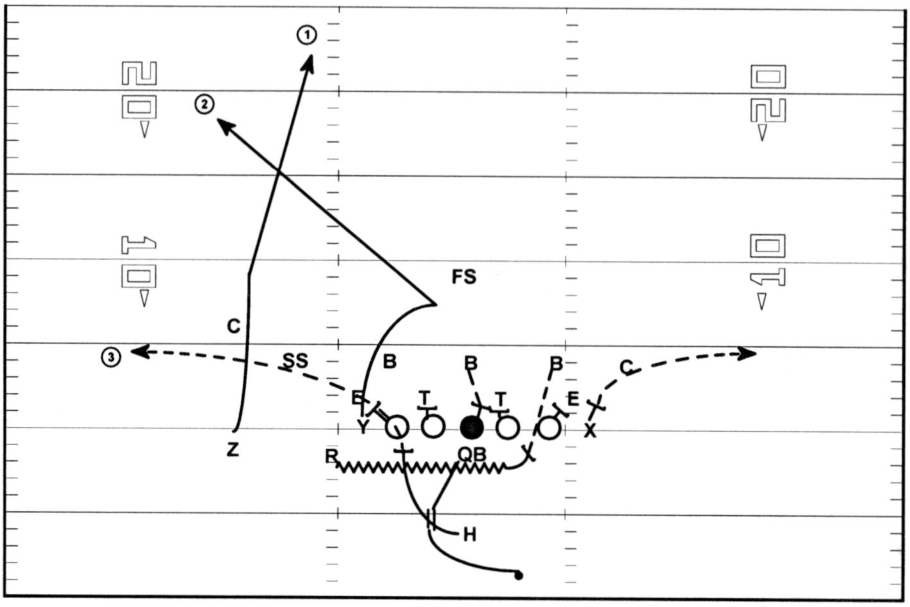

Description: This deep play-action pass off of the inside zone run fake utilizes a short yardage personnel grouping. This play is best utilized into the boundary with a three-layered vertical stretch.

Assignments:

QB: Open fakes inside zone left. Carries out naked (sets up seven to nine yards behind the OT).

H: Executes inside zone left track (great fake). Checks protection. Releases on a flat route.

R: Motions across to B gap. Carries out protection—checks first linebacker inside to outside defender (no pressure—stays in and helps).

Y: Releases best. Executes a throwback route (8 yards to angle at 22 yards).

Z: Aligns six-yard split from Y. Executes a skinny post route.

X: Releases outside. Checks protection (edge pressure). Releases on a flat route.

LT: Executes PAP protection (inside zone).

LG: Executes PAP protection (inside zone).

C: Executes PAP protection (inside zone).

RG: Executes PAP protection (inside zone).

RT: Executes PAP protection (inside zone).

Coaching Points: The QB read progression is Z (post) to Y (throwback route) to H (flat).

Play #69: Unbalanced Zone Left Naked Right Sail

Charlie Stubbs
University of Louisville

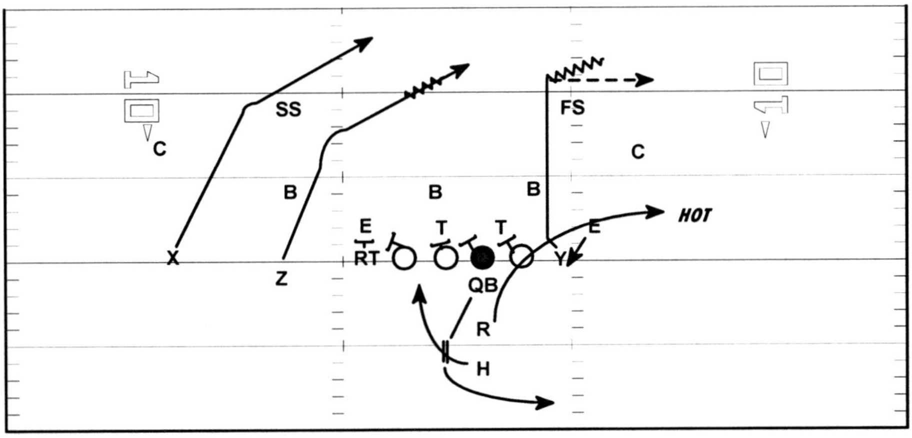

Description: This play is a basic naked out of tackle over an unbalanced formation. This play is a great play in short yardage situations which causes alignment confusion by the defense. It is a good idea to line up in a hurry and use a quick cadence.

Assignments:

QB: Open fakes zone left. Carries out naked (gets depth).

H: Executes inside zone left track.

R: Releases on arrow route (depth two to three yards). Fakes block.

Y: Releases inside. Executes a sail route (depth 12 to 14 yards).

Z: Executes an over route.

X: Executes a post route (replaces the FS).

LT: Executes PAP protection (zone naked).

LG: Executes PAP protection (zone naked).

C: Executes PAP protection (zone naked).

RG: Executes PAP protection (zone naked).

RT: Aligns unbalanced tackle over. Executes PAP protection (zone naked).

Coaching Points: QB must be prepared for quick edge pressure. The QB reads versus pressure is R to Y (low to high). The read for no pressure is Y to R (high to low).

Play #70: Fake Speed Sweep Zone Naked Right Sail

Charlie Stubbs
University of Tulsa

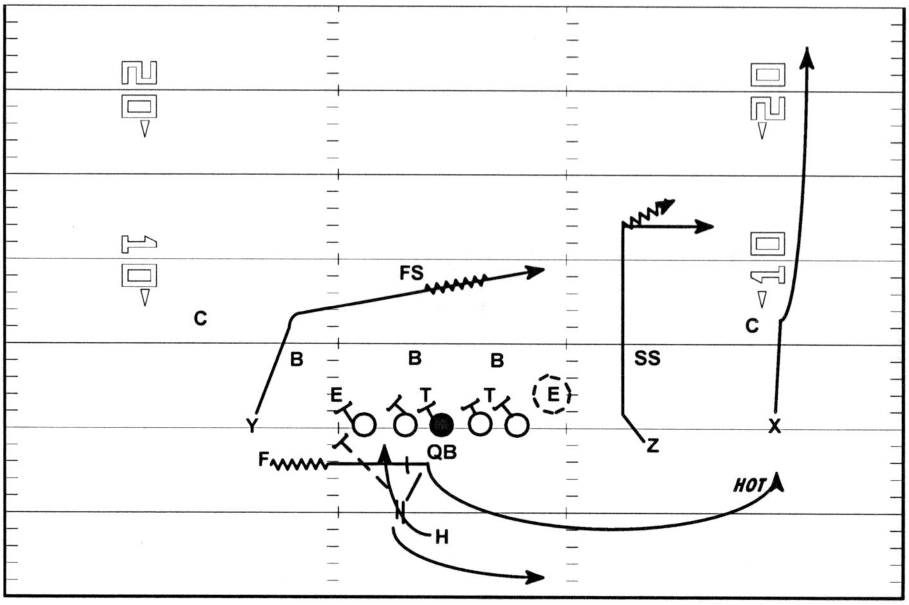

Description: This play complements the speed sweep and inside zone with a play-action pass. A flood route is used toward the strongside.

Assignments:

QB: Open fakes speed sweep then inside zone. Carries out naked (gets depth).

H: Fakes inside zone left. Blocks possible edge pressure.

F: Motions inside. Fakes speed sweep. Bubbles (gets depth). Possible hot receiver.

Y: Executes a crossing route.

Z: Releases inside. Executes a sail route (12 to 14 yards deep).

X: Releases outside on a go route.

LT: Executes PAP protection (zone naked).

LG: Executes PAP protection (zone naked).

C: Executes PAP protection (zone naked).

RG: Executes PAP protection (zone naked).

RT: Executes PAP protection (zone naked).

Coaching Points: The QB must be prepared for quick edge pressure. QB read versus pressure is F (hot). The read with no pressure is X to Z to F (high to low).

Play #71: Zone Left Naked Right Tube

Charlie Stubbs
University of Louisville

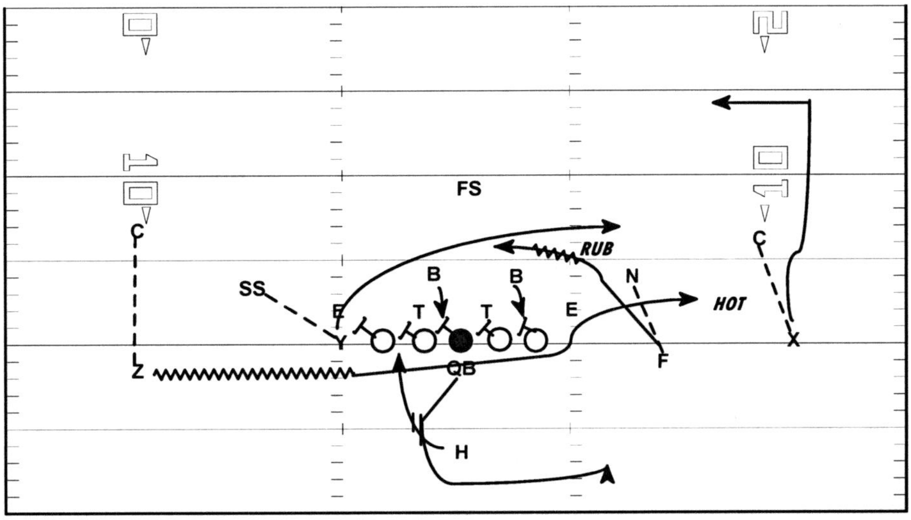

Description: In the naked concept, tube refers to the WR (F) rubbing the defender covering Z. This play is great versus man coverage in the red zone or short yardage situations.

Assignments:

QB: Open fakes inside zone left. Carries out naked (gets depth).

H: Executes inside zone track (great fake).

F: Releases inside. Rubs for Z.

Y: Executes a cross route (depth 8 to 10 yards).

Z: Motions inside to TE/tackle gap (pauses). Releases underneath and runs an arrow route. Hot receiver.

X: In the red zone/goal line area, releases outside on a whirly bird route.

LT: Executes PAP protection (zone naked).

LG: Executes PAP protection (zone naked).

C: Executes PAP protection (zone naked).

RG: Executes PAP protection (zone naked).

RT: Executes PAP protection (zone naked).

Coaching Points: QB must be prepared and expect pressure (gets depth). Z must avoid defenders behind the LOS. The QB progression is Z to Y.

Play #72: Fake Speed Sweep Left Naked Right

Charlie Stubbs
University of Tulsa

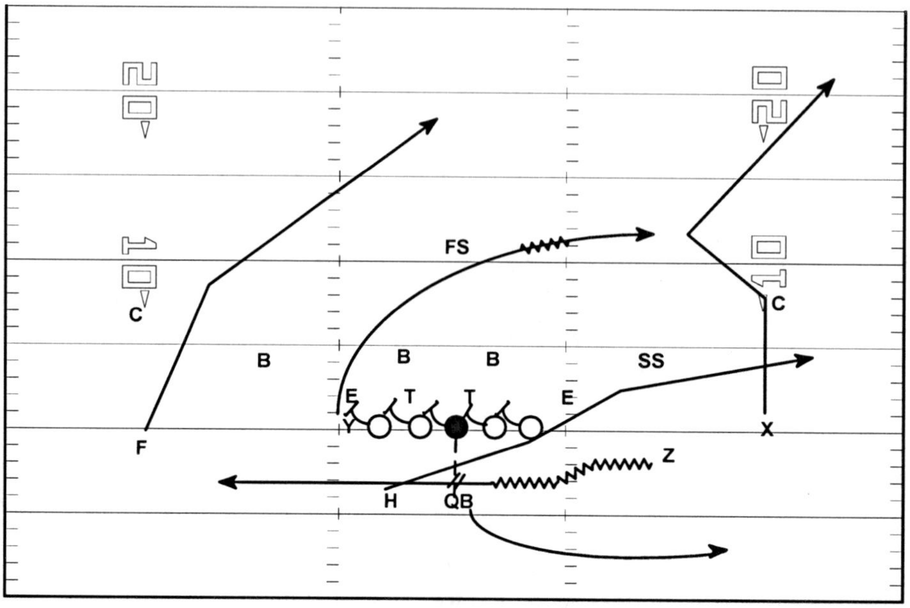

Description: This great play-action pass complements the speed sweep package, attacking a fast flowing defense.

Assignments:

QB: Aligns in gun, faking the speed sweep to Z. Executes a naked right.

H: Aligns at four yards depth and executes an arrow route.

F: Executes a post route and replaces the free safety.

Y: Executes an over route (depth 8 to 10 yards).

Z: Executes inside motion and runs speed sweep left with a great fake.

X: Executes a post corner route.

LT: Executes PAP protection (speed sweep naked).

LG: Executes PAP protection (speed sweep naked).

C: Executes PAP protection (speed sweep naked).

RG: Executes PAP protection (speed sweep naked).

RT: Executes PAP protection (speed sweep naked).

Coaching Points: The QB must be prepared for quick edge pressure. The QB read versus pressure is low to high (H to Y). With no pressure the read is high to low (X to Y to H).

Play #73: Zone Left Naked Right Throwback

Charlie Stubbs
University of Alabama

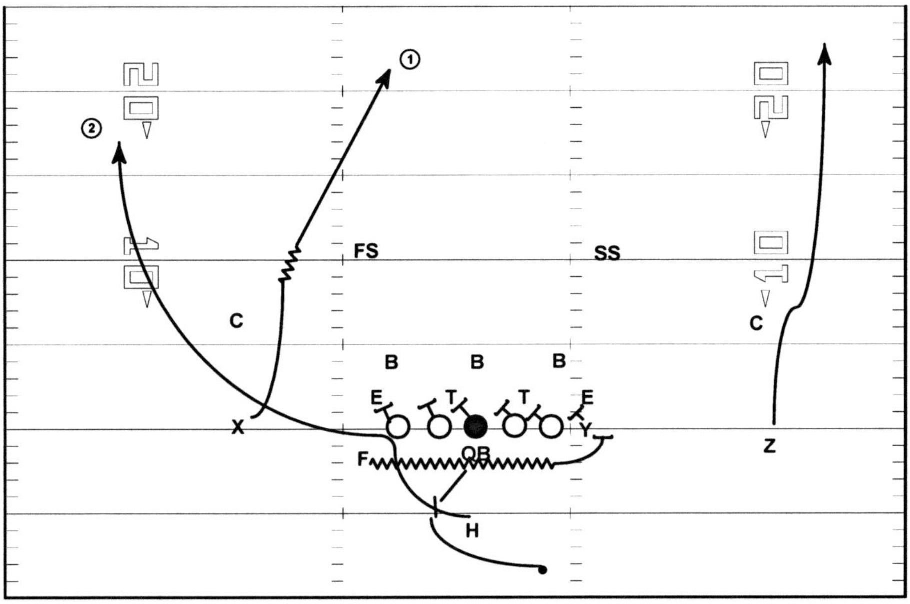

Description: This down the field play-action pass utilizes the wheel route concept. The halfback (H) must be a gifted pass receiver.

Assignments:

QB: Open fakes inside zone left. Naked right. Sets up seven yards behind the OT.

H: Fakes inside zone. Executes wheel route.

F: Executes fly motion. Protection (D gap).

Y: Executes gap protection (Liz).

Z: Releases outside on go route.

X: Executes a stutter post route.

LT: Executes gap protection (Liz).

LG: Executes gap protection (Liz).

C: Executes gap protection (Liz).

RG: Executes gap protection (Liz).

RT: Executes gap protection (Liz).

Coaching Points: The QB progression is X (post) to H (wheel).

7

Special Formation Plays: Bunch, Stack, Empty

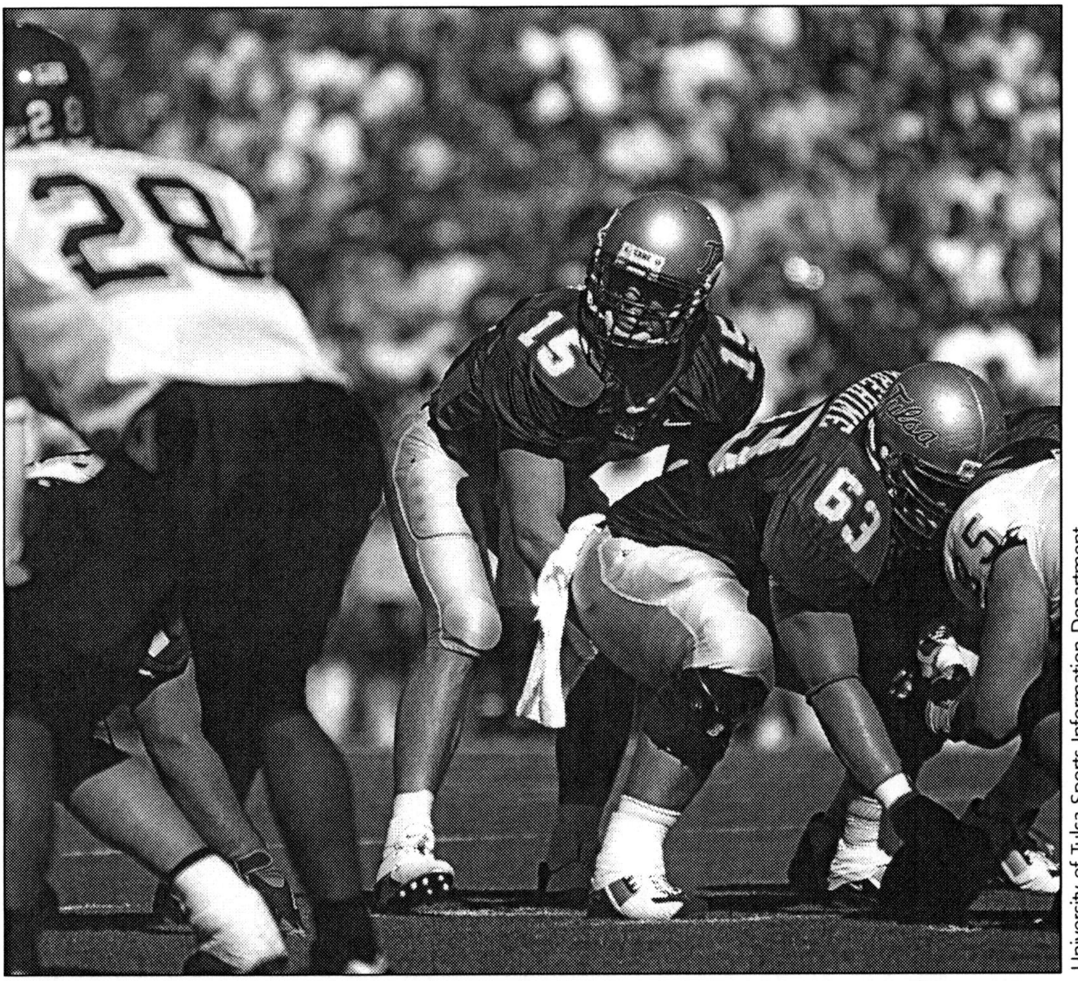

University of Tulsa Sports Information Department

Play #74: Bunch Right Zone Right Fake Reverse Pass Z Over

Noel Mazzone
North Carolina State University

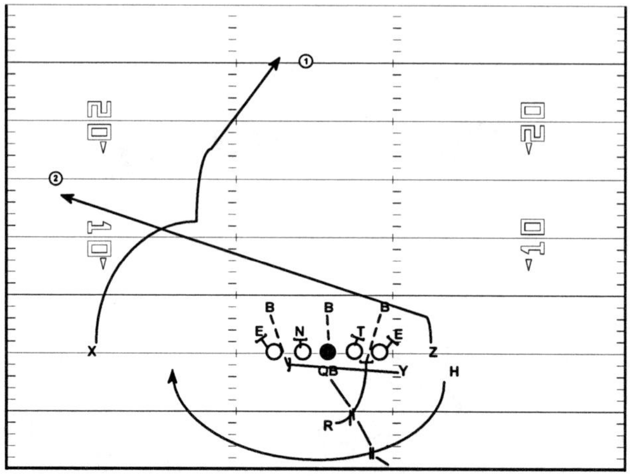

Description: This deep down field play-action pass complements the bunch package. It provides excellent misdirection fakes and attacks the weakside coverage.

Assignments:

QB: Open fakes zone right. Then fakes reverse to H. Gains ground. Sets up in C gap (9 to 10 yards deep).

H: Runs reverse track. Possible hot receiver versus blitz.

R: Runs inside zone track right. Protections inside linebacker to outside (double read). Great fake.

Y: Releases horizontally underneath QB's path. Protections inside linebacker to outside (double read) weakside.

Z: Executes an over route. Responsible for the mesh rub with X.

X: Executes a stalk post route. Responsible for the depth of the mesh (approximately 12 to 15 yards).

LT: Executes PAP protection (big on big).

LG: Executes PAP protection (big on big).

C: Executes PAP protection. Blocks head-up to the left side.

RG: Executes PAP protection (big on big).

RT: Executes PAP protection (big on big).

Coaching Points: The QB progression is X to Z to H. Reminder: H is hot after the reverse fake. Aggressive PAP protection is a must.

Play #75: Bunch Right Zone Right Fake Reverse Pass X Over

Noel Mazzone
North Carolina State University

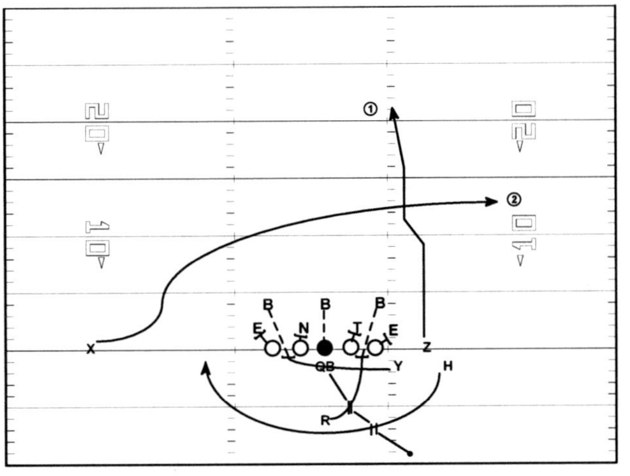

Description: This deep down field play-action pass complements the bunch package. It provides excellent misdirection fakes and attacks the strongside coverage.

Assignments:

QB: Open fakes zone right. Then fakes reverse to H. Gains ground. Sets up in C gap (9 to 10 yards deep).

H: Runs reverse track. Possible hot receiver versus blitz. Great fake.

R: Runs inside zone track right. Protections inside linebacker to outside (double read). Great fake.

Y: Releases horizontally underneath QB's path. Protections inside linebacker to outside (double read) weakside.

Z: Executes a stalk post route. Responsible for the depth of the mesh (approximately 12 to 15 yards).

X: Executes an over route. Splits (five yards). Responsible for the mesh rub with Z.

LT: Executes PAP protection (big on big).

LG: Executes PAP protection (big on big).

C: Executes PAP protection. Blocks head-up to the left side.

RG: Executes PAP protection (big on big).

RT: Executes PAP protection (big on big).

Coaching Points: The QB progression is Z to X to H. Reminder: H is hot after the reverse fake. Aggressive PAP is a must.

Play #76: Bunch Zone Right Reverse Left

Charlie Stubbs
University of Central Missouri

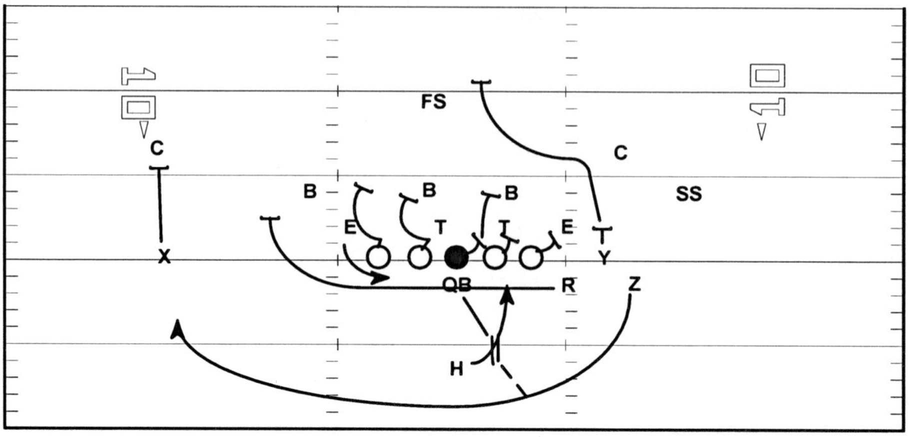

Description: This play provides great misdirection out of the bunch alignment with a very sound blocking scheme.

Assignments:

QB: Open fakes inside zone right. Pitches to Z on reverse.

H: Executes inside zone right track (great fake).

R: Executes horizontal track, avoiding the defensive end. Blocks the weakside support defender.

Y: Slams. Convoy blocks to the middle third of secondary.

Z: Aligns in bunch. Executes reverse track. Secures the pitch and gets depth.

X: Blocks man on.

LT: Steps inside gap. Releases and blocks second level flow.

LG: Slams. Releases and blocks second level flow.

C: Blocks inside zone right.

RG: Blocks inside zone right.

RT: Blocks inside zone right.

Coaching Points: Z (reverse receiver) must get depth to avoid backside edge pressure and read the key block by R.

Play #77: Stack Formation Smash Route

Charlie Stubbs
University of Alabama

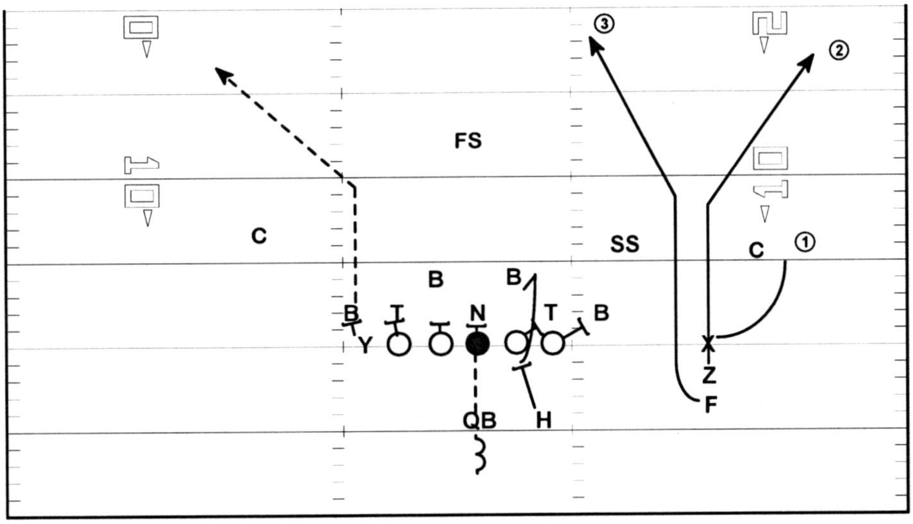

Description: Using this play, an offense using a quick cadence can gain an advantage over a defense's tendencies versus stack alignments.

Assignments:

QB: Utilizes gun alignment or five-step drop.

H: Checks protection. Double reads. Releases on hook route (three yards).

F: Aligns in stack. Stems inside on post route.

Y: Checks protection. Releases on corner route.

Z: Aligns in stack. Executes corner route.

X: Executes smash route (depth five yards).

LT: Executes dropback protection (five step).

LG: Executes dropback protection (five step).

C: Executes dropback protection (five step).

RG: Executes dropback protection (five step).

RT: Executes dropback protection (five step).

Coaching Points: The QB progression is X to Z to F. X is hot on the smash route. The stack alignment should be between the hash and the top of the numbers.

Play #78: Stack Special

Charlie Stubbs
University of Alabama

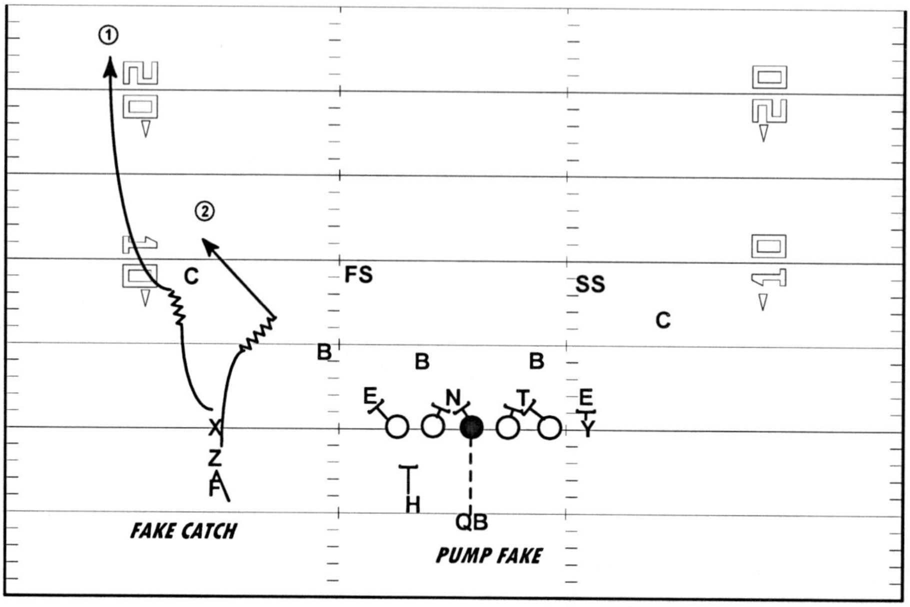

Description: This play is set up by throwing to F with X/Z blocking (similar to WR rules) with an extended handoff. When a defense becomes very aggressive and overpursues, utilize this special play.

Assignments:

QB: Aligns in gun.

H: Checks protection. Helps (maximize protection).

F: Aligns in stack. Fakes catch on stop route (flash hands).

Y: Checks protection. Helps (maximize protection).

Z: Aligns in stack. Releases inside. Fakes block. Executes crack corner route (is patient).

X: Aligns in stack. Executes a stalk and go route (is patient).

LT: Executes a dropback protection (five step).

LG: Executes a dropback protection (five step).

C: Executes a dropback protection (five step).

RG: Executes a dropback protection (five step).

RT: Executes a dropback protection (five step).

Coaching Points: QB pump fakes to F on the stop route. Then reads go route (X) to corner route (Z). The stack alignment should be between the hash and the top of the numbers.

Play #79: No-Back Quick Pass

Charlie Stubbs
University of Alabama

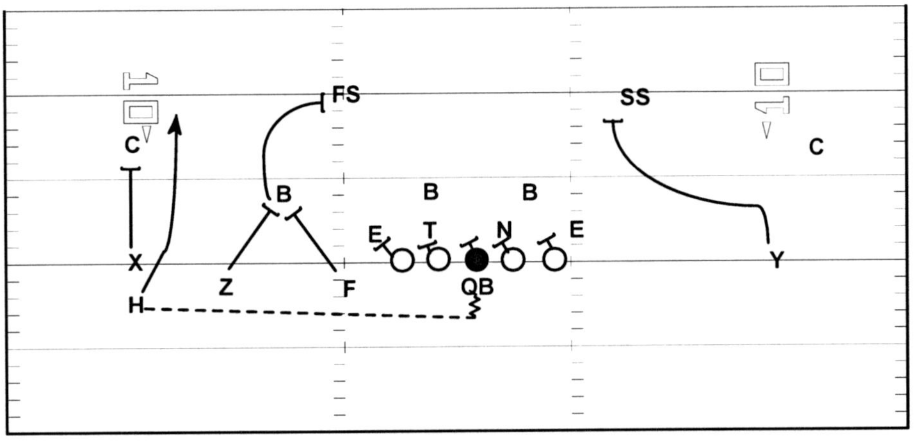

Description: This play has big play potential and is great on first down. With an empty backfield, it can be a high percentage play based on the defense's alignment.

Assignments:

QB: Aligns in gun or underneath center.

H: Stacks behind X. Executes a stop route.

F: Blocks most dangerous defender. Combos to near safety.

Y: Releases inside. Blocks support defender.

Z: Blocks most dangerous defender. Combos to near safety.

X: Blocks man on.

LT: Executes dropback protection (three step).

LG: Executes dropback protection (three step).

C: Executes dropback protection (three step).

RG: Executes dropback protection (three step).

RT: Executes dropback protection (three step).

Coaching Points: If the defense does not displace, the QB will throw the ball to H (stacked WR). If the defense displaces (spreads out), the play will change to a QB draw.

Play #80: Empty—Three-Man Seams

Homer Smith
UCLA/University of Alabama

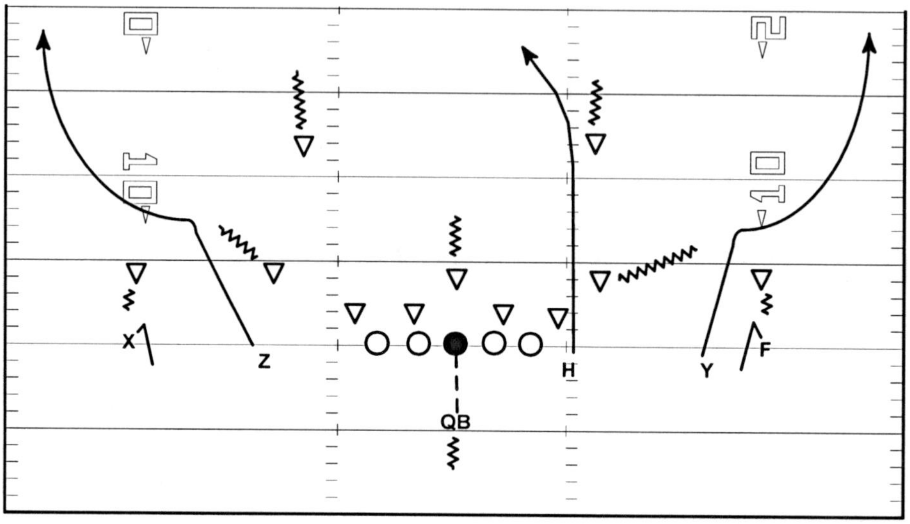

Description: The basic concept of this play is attacking cover 2. The three inside receivers run past the linebackers and put three receivers on two defenders. Expanding routes lets the ball be thrown sooner, over the inside shoulder. The middle receiver runs a divide route, so a ball to him will bisect the field.

Assignments:

QB: Aligns in gun.

H: Executes a divide route (bisects the field).

F: Executes a quick screen route.

Y: Executes an expanding fade route.

Z: Executes an expanding fade route.

X: Executes a quick screen route.

LT: Executes empty pass protection.

LG: Executes empty pass protection.

C: Executes empty pass protection.

RG: Executes empty pass protection.

RT: Executes empty pass protection.

Coaching Points: The QB progression versus cover 2 is H (divide) to Z or Y (expanding fades) to X or F (quick screen).

Play #81: Empty Pass Double Cross

Charlie Stubbs
University of Central Missouri

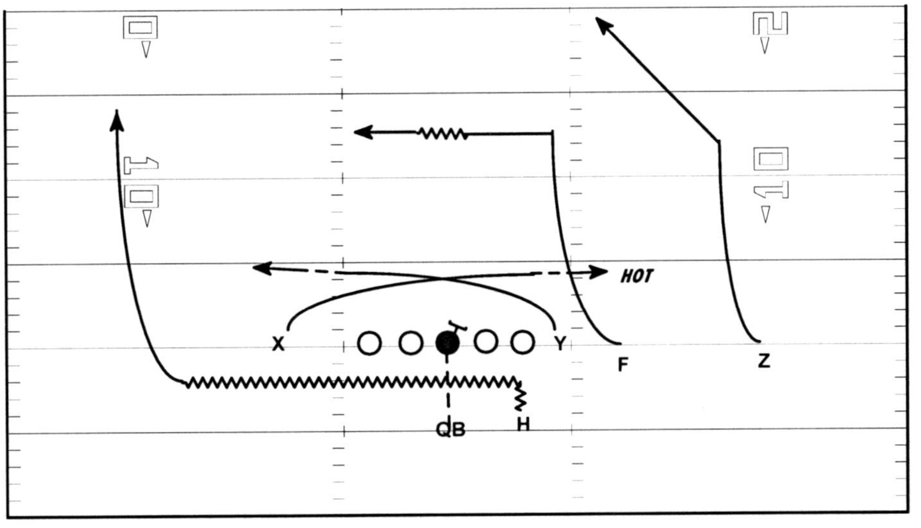

Description: This play builds an empty formation with running back motion. It is a great route versus zone/man/blitz coverage. The built in hot principle is X.

Assignments:

QB: Aligns in gun.

H: Motions wide left. Executes a go route.

F: Executes a wrap around route (12 to 14 yards).

Y: Executes best release on drag route (four to six yards). Responsible for depth of route.

Z: Executes a post route.

X: Aligns five to seven yards split. Executes a drive route. Responsible for mesh (rub). X is hot.

LT: Executes empty protection.

LG: Executes empty protection.

C: Executes empty protection.

RG: Executes empty protection.

RT: Executes empty protection.

Coaching Points: The QB progression in zone coverage reads Z (wrap) to Y/X (mesh). The progression in man/blitz coverage reads X (drive) hot. He should key the post (Z) only if the free safety is aligned tight.

Play #82: Empty Pass Takeoff Y Drive

Charlie Stubbs
University of Central Missouri

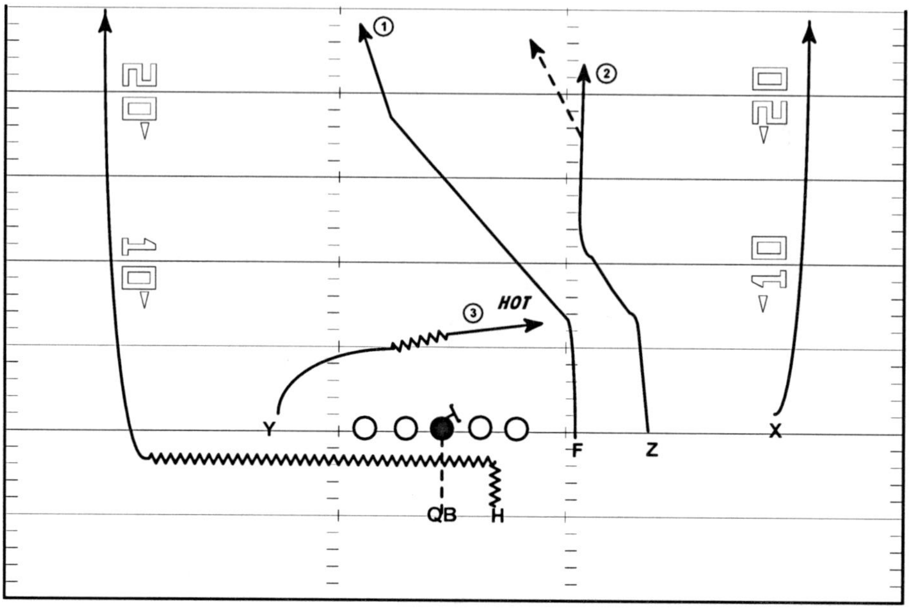

Description: This play builds an empty formation with running back motion. It has a great combination route: four vertical seams with a built in hot principal Y.

Assignments:

QB: Aligns in gun.

H: Motions wide left. Executes a go route.

F: Executes a seam route (landmark is the far hash).

Y: Aligns five to seven yard split. Executes a drive route. Y is hot.

Z: Executes a seam route (down the near hash). Note: cover 2 bends at 18 to 20 yards.

X: Executes a go route (landmark base of the numbers).

LT: Executes empty protection.

LG: Executes empty protection.

C: Executes empty protection.

RG: Executes empty protection.

RT: Executes empty protection.

Coaching Points: The QB progression in zone coverage is F to Z to Y. The progression in man/blitz coverage is Y (drive) hot receiver.

Play #83: Bench and Up Pass

Charlie Stubbs
University of Alabama

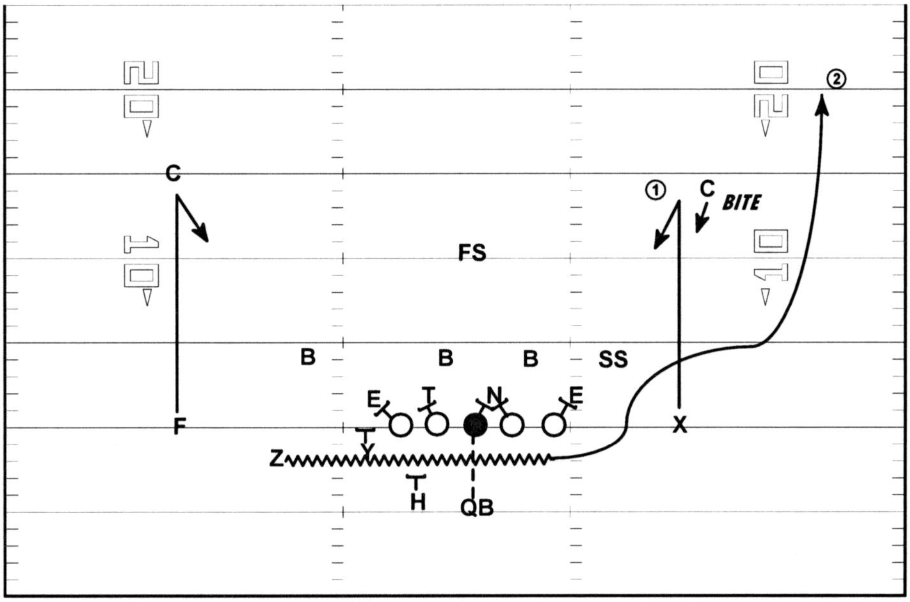

Description: This pass play uses the bench and up pattern and is great versus aggressive cornerback play.

Assignments:

QB: Utilizes gun alignment.

H: Checks protection. Helps (maximize protection).

F: Runs a 14-yard curl route.

Y: Checks protection. Helps (maximize protection).

Z: Utilizes zoom motion. Executes bench and up route.

X: Runs a 14-yard curl route (10 to 12 yard split).

LT: Executes dropback protection (five yards).

LG: Executes dropback protection (five yards).

C: Executes dropback protection (five yards).

RG: Executes dropback protection (five yards).

RT: Executes dropback protection (five yards).

Coaching Points: The QB progression is X to Z on a bench and up route.

Play #84: H Wheel

Charlie Stubbs
University of Alabama

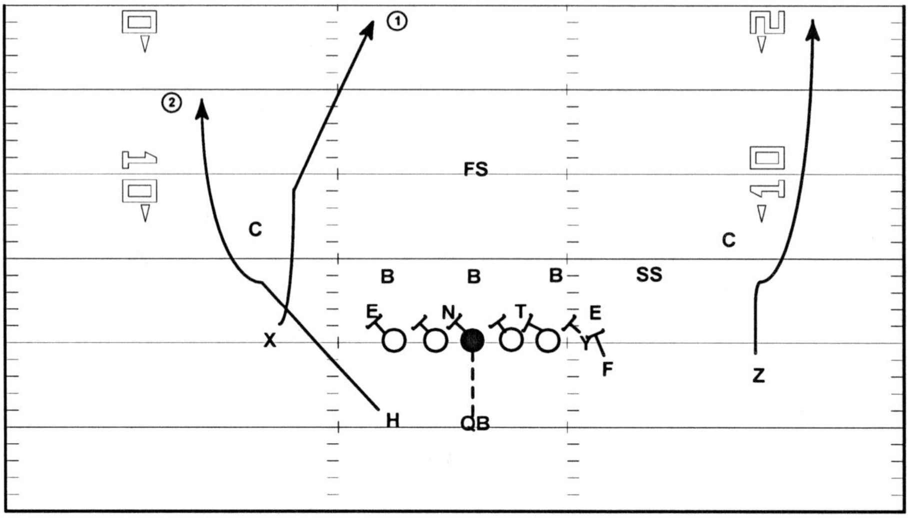

Description: This play is great versus man coverage and can create a mismatch with a playmaker (H) against a linebacker.

Assignments:

QB: Aligns in gun.

H: Aligns behind OT (depth five yards). Executes wheel route.

F: Executes gap protection. D gap.

Y: Executes gap protection (Liz).

Z: Releases outside on go route.

X: Runs a 'skinny' post (break point eight yards).

LT: Executes gap protection (Liz).

LG: Executes gap protection (Liz).

C: Executes gap protection (Liz).

RG: Executes gap protection (Liz).

RT: Executes gap protection (Liz).

Coaching Points: The QB progression is X (skinny post) to H (wheel route.).

8

Special Run Plays

University of Central Missouri Sports Information Department

Play #85: Speed Sweep Right

Charlie Stubbs
University of Tulsa

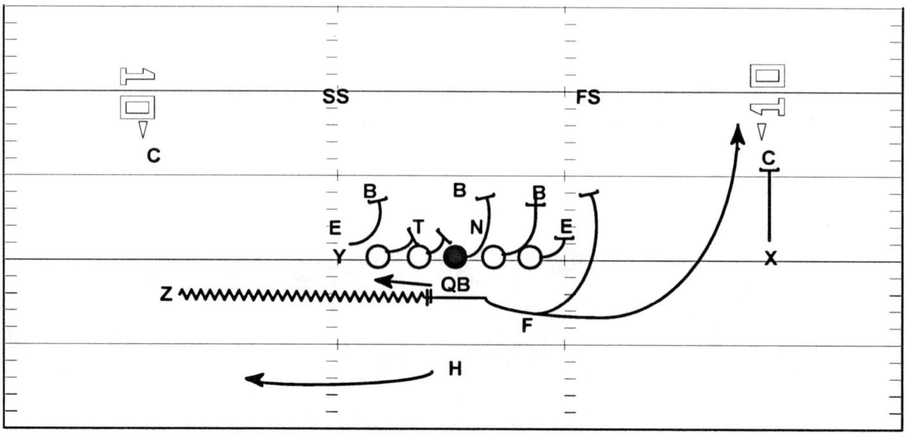

Description: This play offers a great opportunity to utilize wide receivers as ball carriers. It has a very basic blocking scheme using the outside zone technique.

Assignments:

QB: Opens. Hands off speed sweep. Carries out speed option track opposite.

H: Executes speed option track.

F: Blocks outside zone right rules.

Y: Blocks outside zone right rules.

Z: Motions (uses speed). Secures handoff to stretch the defense.

X: Blocks man on.

LT: Blocks outside zone right rules.

LG: Blocks outside zone right rules.

C: Blocks outside zone right rules.

RG: Blocks outside zone right rules.

RT: Blocks outside zone right rules.

Coaching Points: Z (speed sweep runner) must bubble after securing the handoff to avoid edge pressure.

Play #86: T Right Load Option Left

Charlie Stubbs
University of Alabama

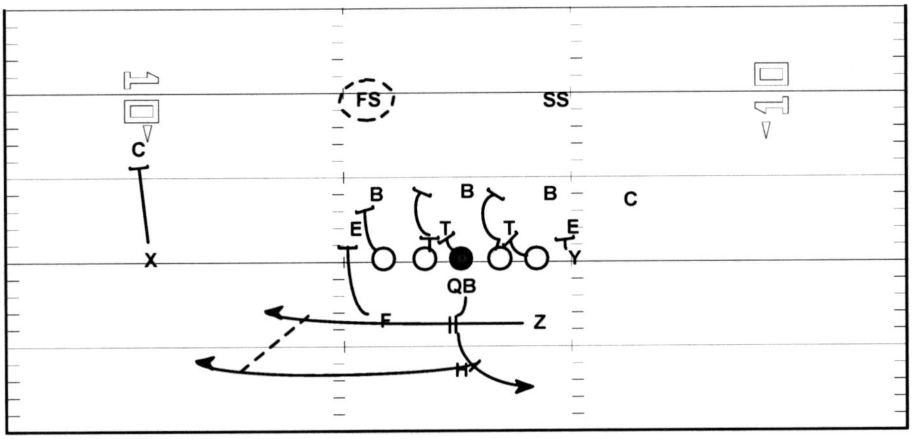

Description: In the T formation executing the load option, the wide receiver (Z) has the opportunity to execute the option phase off of a secondary support defender.

Assignments:

QB: Reverses out. Hands off to Z. Carries out naked fake.

H: Jab steps. Executes option track.

F: Executes load option blocking.

Y: Executes zone blocking.

Z: Executes sweep track. Secures the handoff. Stretches the defense. Executes option phase (run or pitch).

X: Blocks man on.

LT: Executes combo block to second level.

LG: Executes combo block to second level.

C: Executes combo block to second level.

RG: Executes combo block to second level.

RT: Executes combo block to second level.

Coaching Points: The basic blocking rules must be followed with possible cut blocks on the second-level defenders.

Play #87: Bunch Unbalanced Pitch Left

Charlie Stubbs
University of Central Missouri

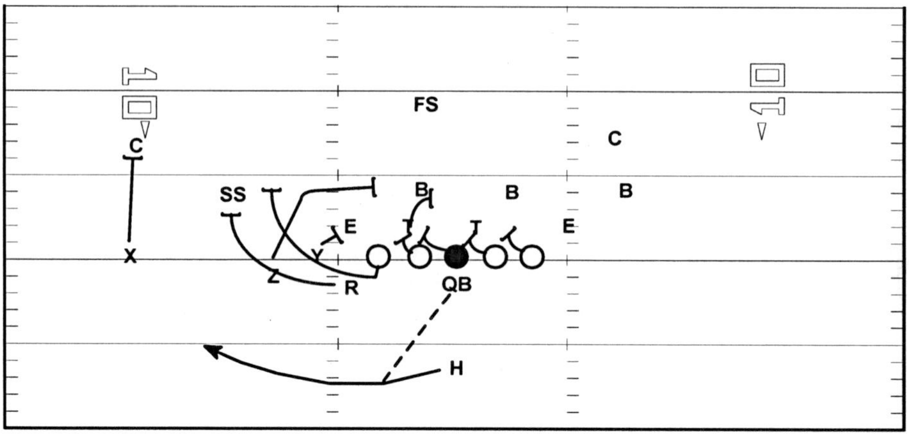

Description: The unbalanced adjustment used in this outside running play will aid in getting an advantage with the blocking scheme. It is a good idea to use a quick cadence.

Assignments:

QB: Reverses out. Executes the pitch to H. Carries out the naked right.

H: Executes pitch left track. Stretches the defense. Runs downhill.

R: Arc releases. Blocks the support defender.

Y: Aligns with a three-yard split. Blocks down. Targets the first defensive lineman inside.

Z: Blocks the first defender inside off of the LOS.

X: Blocks man on. Aligns in unbalanced formation.

LT: Pulls (three strides). Runs downhill and blocks the alley.

LG: Executes combo block to second level.

C: Executes combo block to second level.

RG: Executes zone blocking (inside gap).

RT: Executes zone blocking (inside gap).

Coaching Points: H must take a pre-snap look to anticipate the proper track. Bunch formations cause defenses to adjust alignments.

Play #88: Change 19 (Outside Zone Left)

Charlie Stubbs
University of Central Missouri

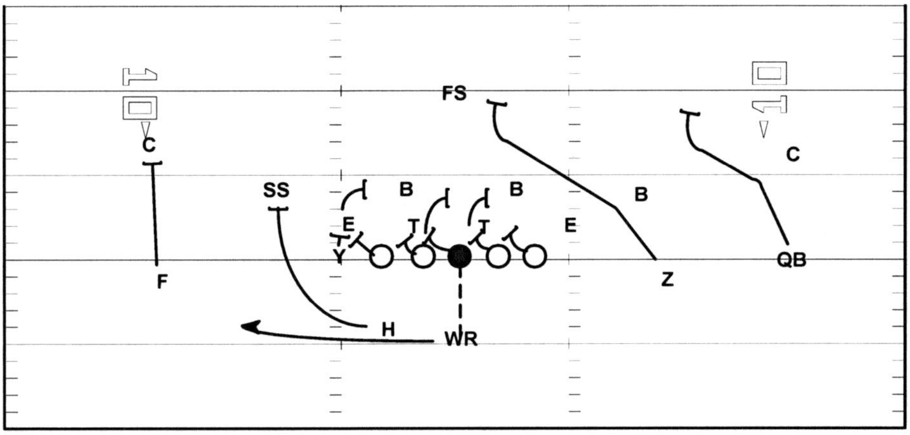

Description: The "change" in this play is switching the playmaker wide receiver and QB's alignment. The single wing offensive philosophy with the outside zone blocking scheme is used with this play.

Assignments:

QB: Says "Change," which alerts the QB to align at a selected wide receiver (X) position.

H: Blocks support defender.

F: Blocks man on.

Y: Executes outside zone left blocking.

Z: Convoys to the middle safety.

X: Aligns in gun. Secures snap. Executes outside zone left track. Change WR.

LT: Executes outside zone left blocking.

LG: Executes outside zone left blocking.

C: Executes outside zone left blocking.

RG: Executes outside zone left blocking.

RT: Executes outside zone left blocking.

Coaching Points: Change receiver (X) should use a basic cadence (set-hut) or silent count if needed.

Play #89: Change 14 (Inside Zone Right)

Charlie Stubbs
University of Central Missouri

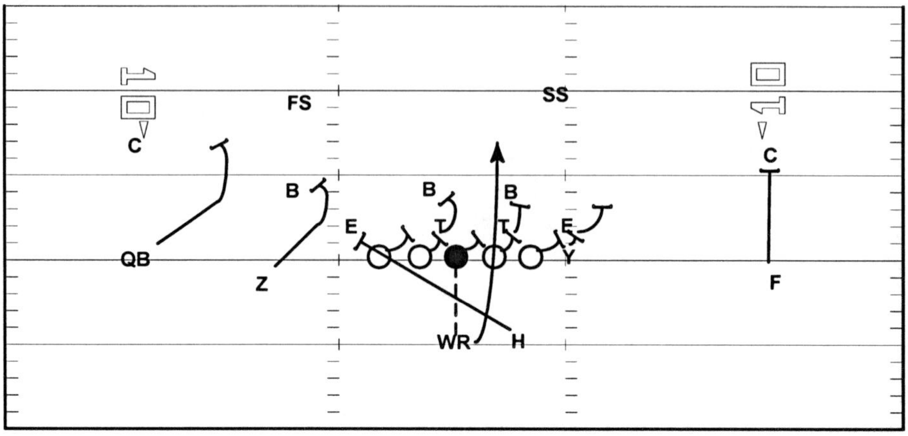

Description: The "change" in this play is switching the playmaker wide receiver and QB's alignment. The single wing offensive philosophy with the inside zone blocking scheme is used with this play.

Assignments:

QB: Says "Change," which alerts the QB to align at a selected wide receiver (X) position.

H: Blocks position cut off on the backside of the inside zone right.

F: Blocks man on.

Y: Executes inside zone right blocking rules.

Z: Blocks most dangerous defender.

X: Aligns in gun. Secures snap. Executes inside zone right track. Change WR.

LT: Executes inside zone right blocking rules.

LG: Executes inside zone right blocking rules.

C: Executes inside zone right blocking rules.

RG: Executes inside zone right blocking rules.

RT: Executes inside zone right blocking rules.

Coaching Points: Change receiver (X) should use a basic cadence (set-hut) or silent count if needed. The ballcarrier should read the first defensive lineman playside to make the proper cut.

Play #90: Zone Read Left Flash

Charlie Stubbs
University of Central Missouri

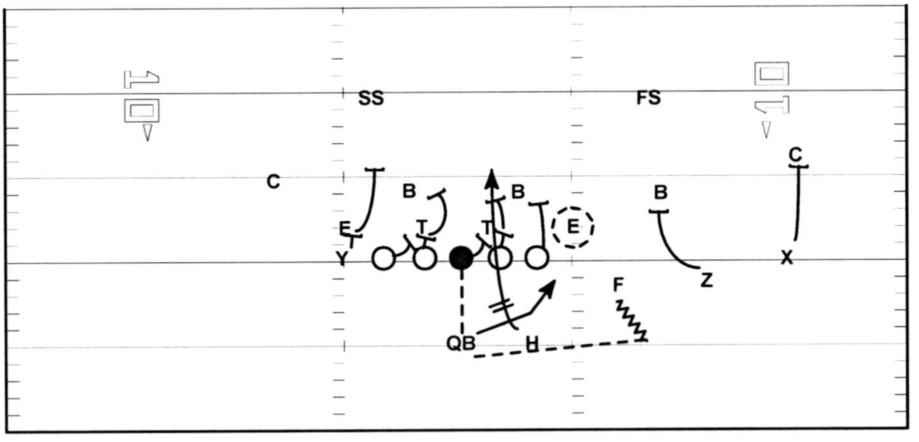

Description: This zone read option variation is used versus a defense that does not displace to spread formations.

Assignments:

QB: Aligns in gun. Executes zone read (give or pull). Possible pass to F (flash).

H: Executes zone read track.

F: Drifts backward from alignment. Stays alert for pass (flash). Runs to daylight.

Y: Slips inside to the high safety.

Z: Blocks most dangerous defender.

X: Blocks man on.

LT: Combo blocks to second level.

LG: Combo blocks to second level.

C: Combo blocks to second level.

RG: Combo blocks to second level.

RT: Climb releases to inside linebacker. Does not block the end man on the LOS.

Coaching Points: The QB will have normal zone read rules to give or pull the ball based on the play of the defensive end. If the QB is forced to pull the ball, he will then drop, step, and throw a pass to F (WR) as he drifts backward.

Play #91: Zone Read Arc

Charlie Stubbs
University of Tulsa

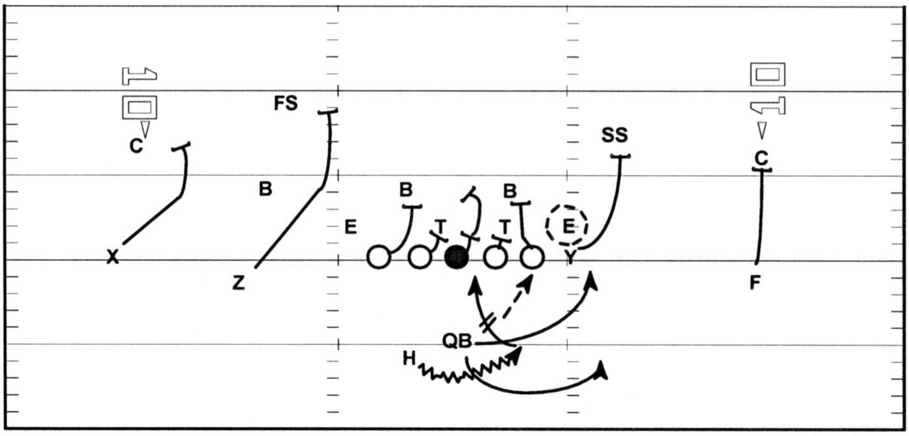

Description: This play is a great running play out of gun alignment. It offers option football with the zone read concept toward the strength of the formation (TE side). Utilizing short running back motion (hip) will aid in disguising this play from defensive recognition.

Assignments:

QB: Aligns in gun. Executes zone read (give or run).

H: Executes short motion (hip) switching side of QB. Executes zone read track.

F: Blocks man on.

Y: Arc releases to block the support defender.

Z: Convoys to the middle third of the secondary.

X: Convoys to the near safety.

LT: Zone blocks.

LG: Combo blocks to second level.

C: Combo blocks to second level.

RG: Combo blocks to second level.

RT: Climb releases to inside linebacker. Does not block the end man on LOS.

Coaching Points: The QB will have the normal zone read rules to give or pull the ball based on the play of the defensive end.

Play #92: Zone Read Option—Ex. 1

Charlie Stubbs
University of Tulsa

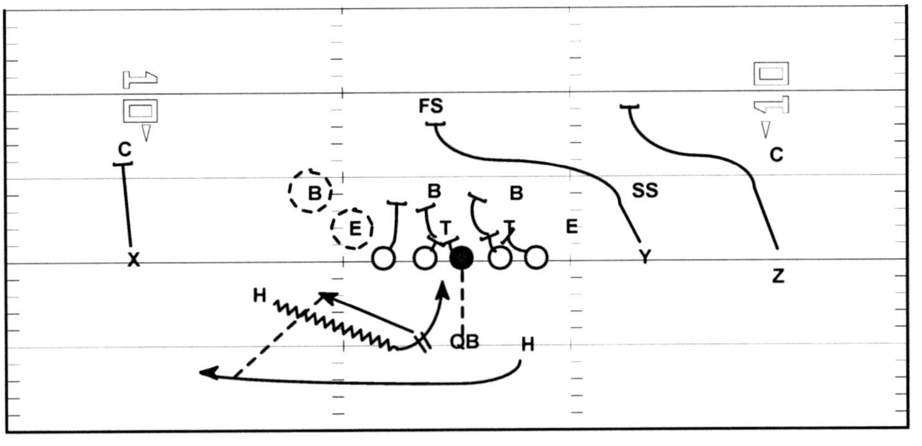

Description: This play is a great running play out of gun alignment. It offers option football with the zone read option concept utilizing two running backs.

Assignments:

QB: Aligns in gun. Executes zone read option.

H: Motions to backfield. Executes zone read track.

H: Executes option phase (possible pitch).

Y: Convoy blocks to the middle safety.

Z: Convoy blocks to the near safety.

X: Blocks man on.

LT: Climb releases to inside linebacker. Does not block the end man on LOS.

LG: Combo blocks to second level.

C: Combo blocks to second level.

RG: Combo blocks to second level.

RT: Combo blocks to second level.

Coaching Points: The QB will execute zone read rules to give or pull the ball based on the play of the defensive end. If it is a pull, the QB will progress to option phase and read a second-level defender (linebacker or safety).

Play #93: Zone Read Option—Ex. 2

Charlie Stubbs
University of Tulsa

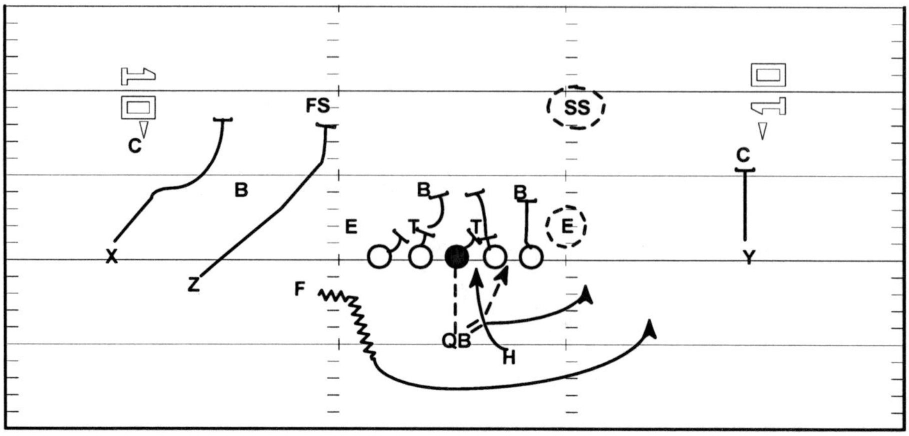

Description: This play is a great running play from gun utilizing a spread alignment. It is excellent versus defenses that do not displace. The scheme makes it possible to handle six defenders in the box with only five blockers (OL). This play is option football with the zone read concept.

Assignments:

QB: Aligns in gun. Executes zone read option.

H: Executes zone read track.

F: Motions to backfield. Must use speed to get into the option phase.

Y: Blocks man on.

Z: Convoy blocks to the near safety.

X: Convoy blocks.

LT: Zone blocks.

LG: Combo blocks to second level.

C: Combo blocks to second level.

RG: Combo blocks to second level.

RT: Climb releases to the inside linebacker. Does not block the end man on LOS.

Coaching Points: The QB will execute zone read rules to give or pull the ball based on the play of the defensive end. If it is a pull, the QB will progress to option phase (F) and read a second-level defender (linebacker or defensive back).

Play #94: Unbalanced Zone Read Option—Ex. 3

Charlie Stubbs
University of Tulsa

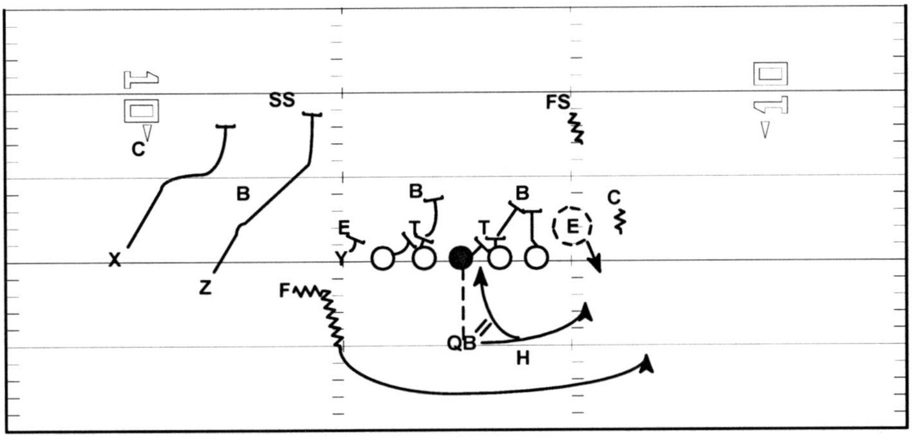

Description: This play is a zone read option out of an unbalanced formation. This alignment will cause defenders to lose their gap responsibilities or spread the defense thin.

Assignments:

QB: Aligns in gun. Executes zone read option.

H: Executes zone read track.

F: Motions to the backfield. Must use speed to get into the option phase.

Y: Blocks man in the inside gap.

Z: Convoy blocks to the near safety.

X: Convoy blocks.

LT: Zone blocks.

LG: Combo blocks to second level.

C: Combo blocks to second level.

RG: Combo blocks to second level.

RT: Climb releases to inside linebacker. Does not block the end man on the LOS.

Coaching Points: The QB will execute zone read rules to give or pull the ball based on the play of the defensive end. If it is a pull, the QB will progress to option phase (F) and read a second-level defender (linebacker or defensive back).

Play #95: Belly Right Flip Left

Charlie Stubbs
University of Central Missouri

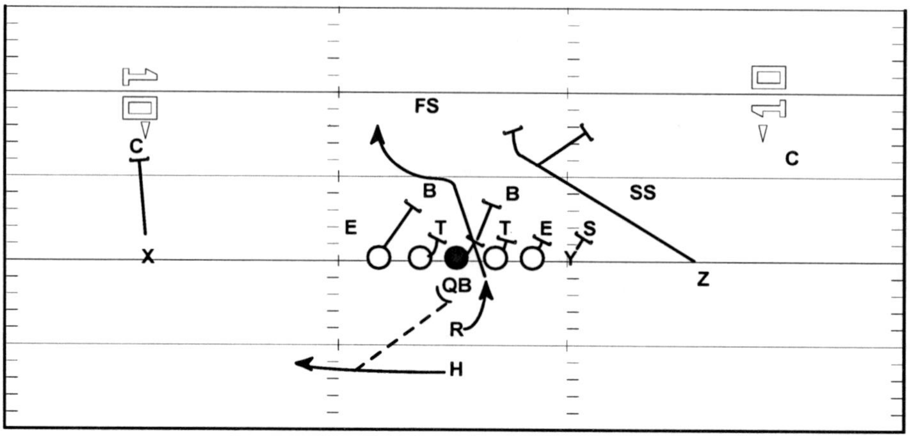

Description: With a visual audible, the QB determines and executes belly or flip.

Assignments:

QB: Reverses out. Possible belly (give) or flip (pitch), based on the defensive alignment.

H: Executes speed option left track.

R: Executes belly right track (possible give).

Y: Blocks inside zone right.

Z: Convoy blocks to the middle third area.

X: Blocks man on.

LT: Blocks inside zone right.

LG: Blocks inside zone right.

C: Blocks inside zone right.

RG: Blocks inside zone right.

RT: Blocks inside zone right.

Coaching Points: The QB will handle all ball handling with a belly give or flip. The decision will be based on the alignment of the defense on the weakside of the offensive formation. When the defenders are wide, the QB will execute the belly and give the ball to R. The QB will flip the ball with a tight defensive alignment.

9

Kicking Game Special Plays and Fakes

University of Tulsa Sports Information Department

Play #96: Punt Team Special

Charlie Stubbs
University of Tulsa

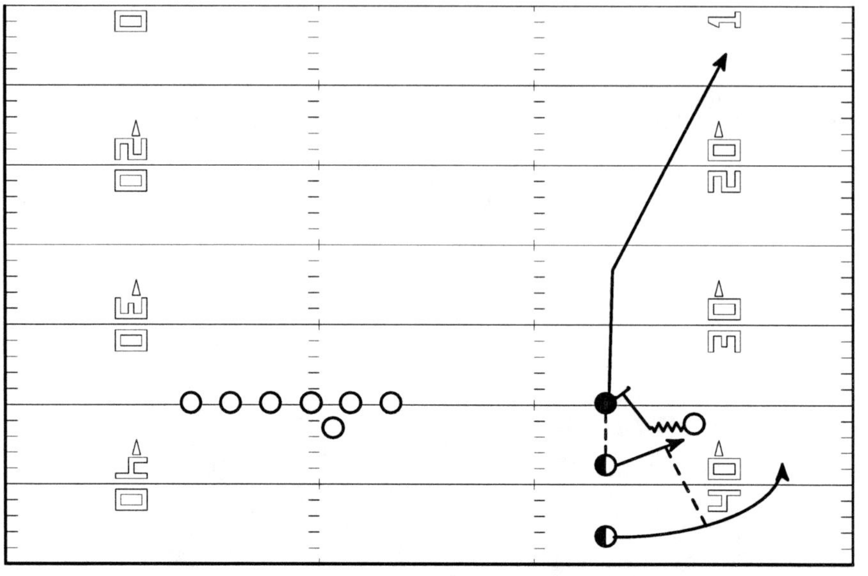

Description: This play utilizes the punt team personnel who must align quickly. It is best called in a fourth-down situation at the +50-yard line with four to six yards needed. The play has a pass or option read.

Assignments:

P: Aligns at eight yards depth. Executes the speed option track.

H: Aligns at four yards depth behind X. Executes speed option or throws corner route to X.

F: Executes short motion. Blocks the defender aligned on X.

Y: Aligns in normal alignment on the left hash.

Z: Aligns on the left hash off the LOS.

X: Aligns between the hash mark and the top of the numbers. Executes the snap. Runs a corner route.

LT: Aligns on the left hash.

LG: Aligns on the left hash.

C: Aligns on the left hash.

RG: Aligns on the left hash.

RT: Aligns on the left hash.

Coaching Points: Personnel groupings and positions may vary based on the available players needed to execute this special play. The following are key points to follow:

- There must be seven offensive players on the LOS.
- The snapper (center) must have an eligible jersey number and executes a corner route.
- The motion receiver must have an eligible jersey number and blocks the defender aligned on the snapper.
- The QB aligns in gun and must make the decision for the pass or run option based on the defense's alignment.
- The running back executes a speed option right track.

Play #97: Reverse Punt Return

Danny Pearman
Virginia Tech University

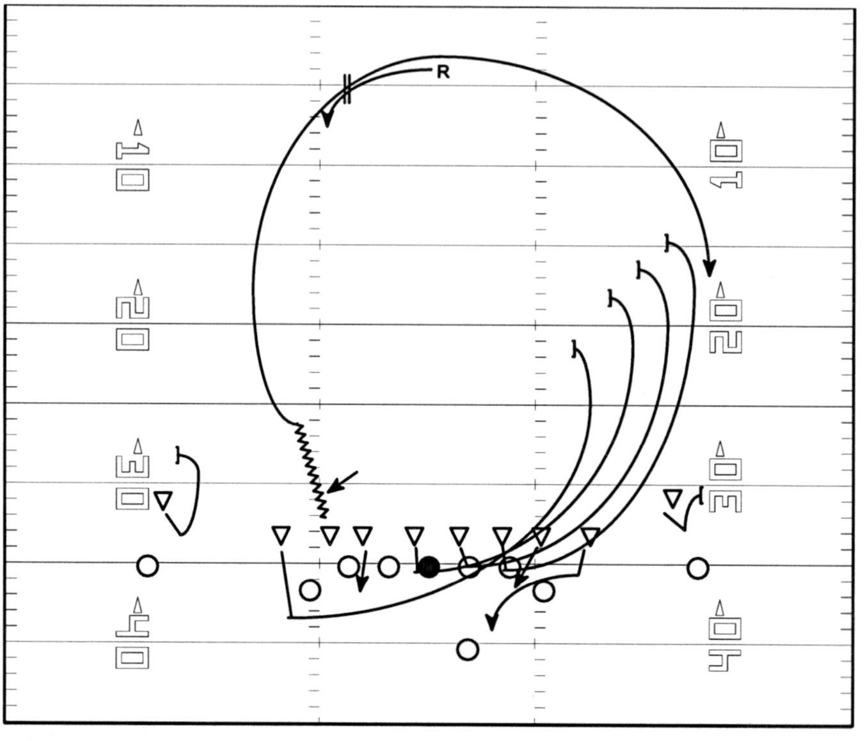

Description: This special team play utilizes a playmaker on the punt return team executing a reverse punt return with a wall blocking scheme.

Assignments:

Defensive Front: Slam releases to set up a wall return.

Cornerbacks: Blocks the strikers.

Playmaker: Releases early out of the front. Retreats quickly to mesh and receives handoff from the returner.

Returner: Secures punt catch. Sprints right to handoff ball to the playmaker for the wall left.

Coaching Points: The playmaker must begin to retreat prior to the snap to sprint back to receive the reverse handoff from the returner. The punt return team will execute a basic wall blocking scheme toward the sideline.

Play #98: Kickoff Return Throwback Pass

Danny Pearman
Virginia Tech University

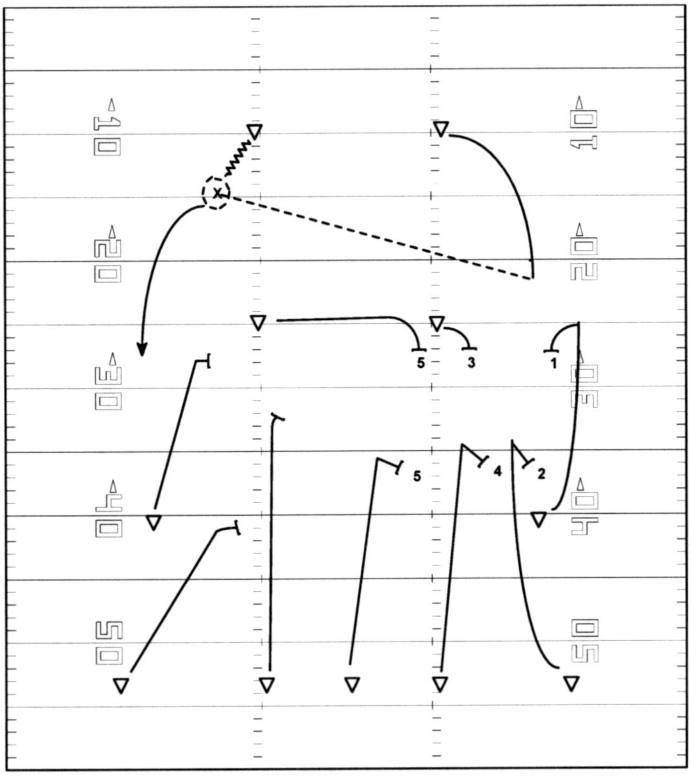

Description: This kickoff return special play utilizes a throwback pass to exploit kickoff coverage teams that do not stay in their coverage lanes.

Assignments:

Front Line: Retreats to field landmarks and executes blocking assignments.

Second Line: Retreats to field landmarks and executes blocking assignments.

Third Line: Sets up for wedge and executes blocking assignments.

Left Returner: Secures kickoff. Returns left and pivots for throwback pass.

Right Returner: Delays on opposite hash. Stays five yards deeper than the returner for a lateral pass.

Coaching Points: After catching the kickoff, the returner must run forward to sell the action, then make the backward (lateral) throw to his teammate. A wall return will be set up to escort the playmaker down the field into the end zone.

Play #99: Fake Field Goal Flood Pattern

Danny Pearman
Virginia Tech University

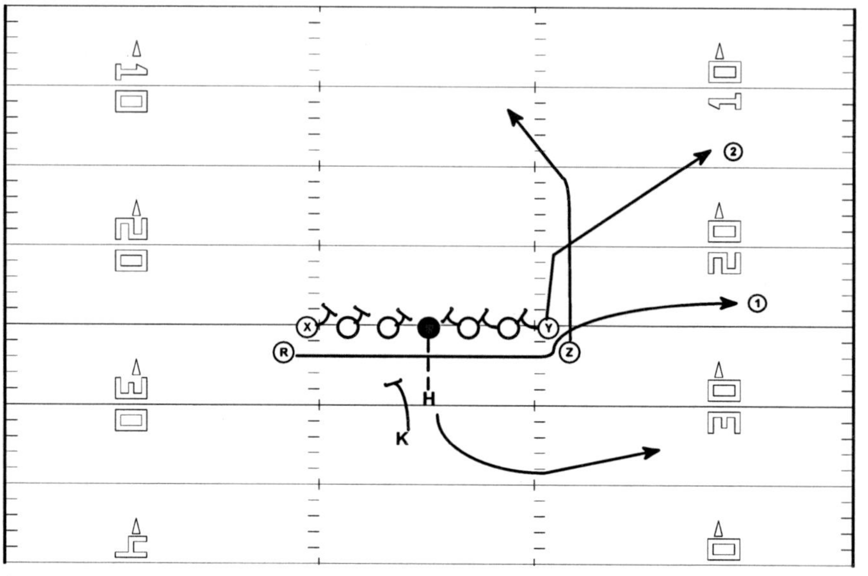

Description: This special play with the field goal team exploits a defense that overloads and pressures from the left side.

Assignments:

Holder: Receives snap and sprints right.

Kicker: Fakes kick and blocks backside pursuit.

R: Runs horizontal behind the LOS and executes an arrow route.

Y: Executes a corner route.

Z: Runs a post route to clear the area for flood pattern.

X: Field goal protection (gap).

LT: Field goal protection (gap).

LG: Field goal protection (gap).

C: Field goal protection (gap).

RG: Field goal protection (gap).

RT: Field goal protection (gap).

Coaching Points: The holder must be quick to arc on the sprint-out action to gain depth. The holder must read R on an arrow route to Y on the corner route. The decision for the holder to run is also an option based on the down, distance, or situation.

Play #100: Fake Field Goal Pass

Scott Grinde
University of Central Missouri

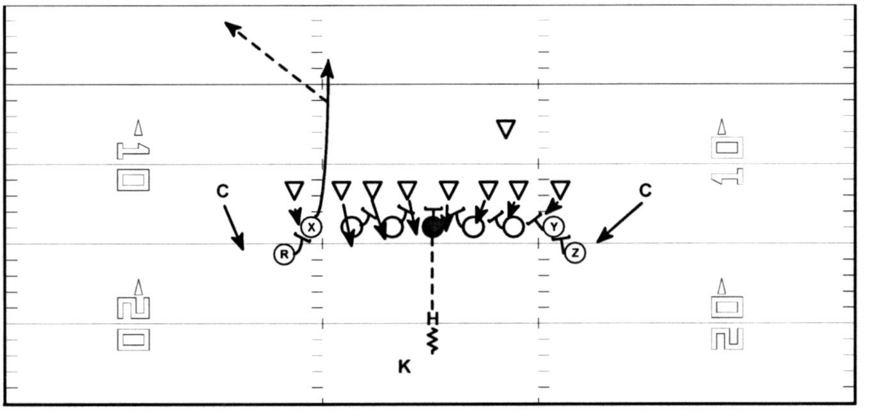

Description: In this special team play, the audible signal sends a receiver out and overloads the coverage. The holder makes a green call, and X runs a seam or corner route based on the coverage.

Assignments:

Holder: Receives the snap and drifts back to execute the pass.

Kicker: Fakes the kick and protects inside to out.

R: Field goal protection (gap).

Y: Field goal protection (gap).

Z: Field goal protection (gap).

X: Executes a seam or corner route based on the coverage.

LT: Field goal protection (gap).

LG: Field goal protection (gap).

C: Field goal protection (gap).

RG: Field goal protection (gap).

RT: Field goal protection (gap).

Coaching Points: The receiver (X) will execute the proper route based on the coverage and game plan.

Play #101: Fake Field Goal Shovel Pass

Scott Grinde
University of Central Missouri

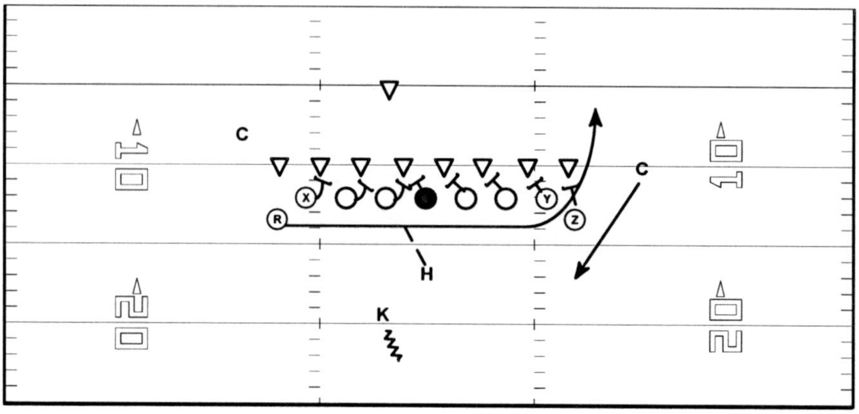

Description: The audible in this special teams play is used for the direction toward the block with Rodeo (right) or Lion (left). It is important that you have the advantage based on the defense's alignment.

Assignments:

Holder: Receives the snap and executes the shovel pass.

Kicker: Fakes a bad snap.

R: Runs horizontal behind the LOS and receives the shovel pass.

Y: Field goal protection (gap).

Z: Field goal protection (gap).

X: Field goal protection (gap).

LT: Field goal protection (gap).

LG: Field goal protection (gap).

C: Field goal protection (gap).

RG: Field goal protection (gap).

RT: Field goal protection (gap).

Coaching Points: The protection must not allow penetration from the defensive front. The shovel pass will be executed from the kneeling holder position.

About the Author

Charlie Stubbs has over two decades of experience as a collegiate assistant coach, including 14 seasons as an offensive coordinator, three years as passing game coordinator, and six years as an assistant head coach, at schools such as Oregon State University, University of Memphis, University of Tennessee-Martin, University of Nevada-Las Vegas, University of Alabama, University of Tulsa, University of Louisville, and University of Central Missouri.

Stubbs began his collegiate coaching career as a graduate assistant on LaVell Edwards' staff at Brigham Young University in 1983, and in 1984 was a member of the BYU coaching staff that led the Cougars to the Division I-A National Championship. At Oregon State, he began as receivers and tight end coach for the 1985 and 1986 seasons before being promoted to offensive coordinator in 1987. The Beavers offenses were ranked among the PAC-10's top three each season in passing offense, and ranked tenth nationally in 1987 and sixth in 1988.

At Tennessee-Martin, the offense in 1995 ranked first in the Ohio Valley Conference in passing offense, ranked fifth nationally in Division I-AA, and established nine new OVC offensive records. The UNLV teams ranked second in the Western Athletic Conference and ninth nationally in passing offense in 1996, while leading the WAC in 1997 and finishing that season ranked twelfth in NCAA statistics.

During his three seasons (1998-2000) at Alabama as passing game coordinator and quarterbacks coach, Alabama played in the 1998 Music City Bowl and the Orange Bowl following the 1999 season. The Crimson Tide was also crowned SEC champions in 1999, and Stubbs was named the 1999 SEC Offensive Coordinator of the Year.

In his first season at Tulsa, the Hurricane offense was ranked 23rd nationally in rushing offense, an improvement of 63 places from the previous year; 28th in scoring offense, a jump of 73 spots from 2002; and 51st in total offense, an improvement of 54 spots from the previous season. The Golden Hurricanes also appeared in the 2003 Humanitarian Bowl.

The 2005 season was very eventful at T.U. The team posted a 9–4 record—winning the Conference USA title versus Central Florida and the Liberty Bowl Championship versus Fresno State. The Golden Hurricane offense led in many conference and NCAA statistical categories. In the 2006 season T.U. posted a record of 8–4 and was invited to the Bell Helicopter Armed Forces Bowl versus the University of Utah.

In four seasons, the Tulsa offense averaged over 31 points per game—more than 50 points in three games, more than 40 points in nine games, and more than 30 points in 16 games—ranking among the Top 25 teams in the country in scoring in each season. While at Tulsa, Stubbs was a finalist for the AFCA Assistant Coach of the Year.

In 2007, the University of Louisville offense was ranked high nationally and was at the top of the Big East Conference in numerous categories: passing offense (first in the Big East and fourth nationally); passing efficiency (second in the Big East and ninth nationally); total offense (first in the Big East and sixth nationally). They ranked 18th in the nation in scoring offense with an average of 35.2 points per game.The 2008 University of Central Missouri offense was very productive under Stubbs. They ranked number one in the MIAA in passing offense, and their offense averaged over 400 yards of total offense, scoring more than 36 points per game.

In Stubbs' career, he has coached nine all-conference quarterbacks and had three quarterbacks earn All-American honors, including Oregon State's Erik Wilhelm and freshman All-Americans Jon Denton of UNLV and Tyler Watts of Alabama.

Stubbs began his collegiate playing career at Wofford College, but after suffering an injury, transferred to BYU. He earned his bachelor's degree in 1978 and his master's degree in 1984, both from BYU.

Stubbs and his wife, Sandy, both originally from Charleston, South Carolina, have four children: Troy, Jay, Kim, and Kyle, two daughters-in-law, Jenny and Mary, and five grandchildren*.